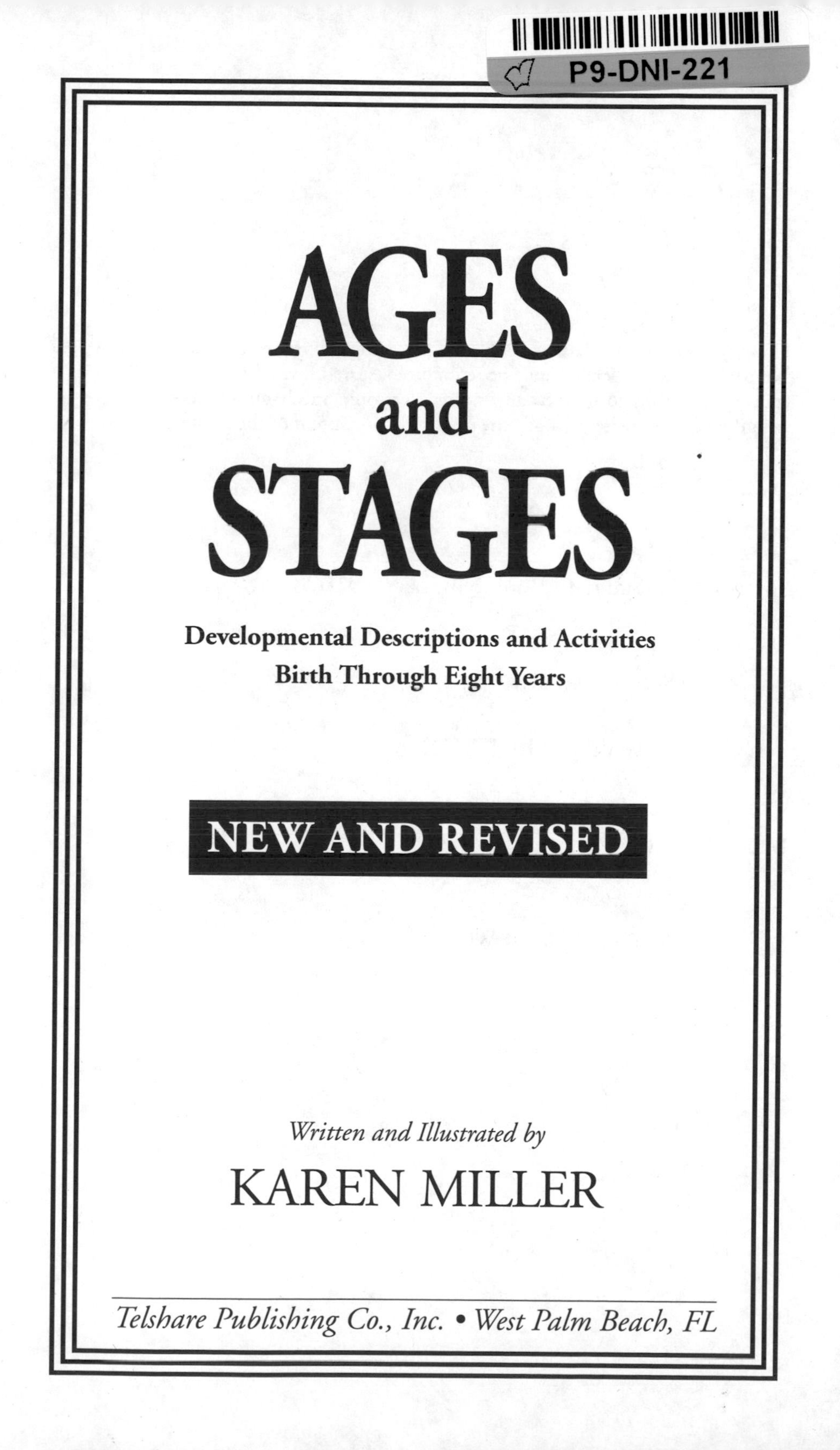

AGES and STAGES

Developmental Descriptions and Activities
Birth Through Eight Years

NEW AND REVISED

Written and Illustrated by

KAREN MILLER

Telshare Publishing Co., Inc. • West Palm Beach, FL

International Standard Book Number: 0-910287-16-3

NEW AND REVISED EDITION

Second Printing: February 2003

Cover Photography: David Woods

DEDICATION

This second edition of AGES AND STAGES is dedicated to Nilea Ogden, my new grandchild, born while this revision was in progress. May you give your mother and father a joyous ride through childhood, and together enjoy all the wonderful ages and stages ahead!

Acknowledgments

I WOULD LIKE TO EXPRESS my appreciation and respect for the hundreds of early childhood caregivers, teachers and family child care providers who have endured my presence in their rooms and have so generously shared their ideas with me over the years. The amount of creative energy and dedication in the field of early childhood education is inspiring. And special thanks go to Nancy Bailey, Lois Dewsnap and Don Dewsnap for their encouragement, advice and editing skills in putting this revised volume together.

Synergism is a wonderful thing!

Contents

CHAPTER 4: THE TWO-YEAR-OLD

Chapter 7: THE FIVE-YEAR-OLD

Introduction

CARING FOR YOUNG CHILDREN is work full of challenges, rewards and surprises. It is the "surprises" part that keeps us interested. Watching young children grow and develop new skills is one of the most rewarding parts of being a parent or a teacher. Keeping children interested and happily occupied while they are learning requires that we know them well.

The primary focus of this book is on how developmental stages and behaviors show up in group child care situations. My remarks and observations are confined to that type of setting. I do not talk about such things as feeding and physical care, bedtime rituals, sibling rivalry and other issues confined mainly to family situations. Recognizing that every parent is part teacher, and every teacher must "parent" or "nurture" children, it is hoped that parents as well as teachers will find information of value in these pages. There is no reason why a parent cannot provide an enriched learning environment in the home, the child's most important setting for learning.

Emerging Skills

If you work with young children, it is useful to understand the concept of "emerging skills." These are capabilities, both physical and mental, that children are almost developing, or have just recently mastered. The interesting thing is that when a skill is new, it is usually "compulsive." Children want to do it again and again and again. This self-imposed drill seems to be a natural learning style for humans.

You see an emerging skill in the infant who loves to crawl up stairs, the toddler who first learns to walk, the two-year-old who learns to name objects, the three-year-old who learns to cut with scissors, the four-year-old who likes to jump off low platforms, the five-year-old who starts to recognize words to read. Incidentally, this phenomenon is not limited to children. Think of the teenager who learns to drive a car, or the adult who learns how to ski.

In planning your program, the trick is to zero in on the emerging skills of the children in your group. Observe them closely to see what they enjoy doing most and seem "driven" to do. Then think of many safe and varied ways they can practice this type of activity, perhaps adding little challenges as time goes on.

Even in groups of children close in age, you will find a lot of variation in children's capabilities and interests. How do you plan activities that will meet the needs of all of them? First of all, many activities and materials, play dough for instance, have a fairly broad range of appeal. Children will use the same materials with different levels of skill and complexity. Secondly, you can set up an environment with many acceptable activities for children to choose from. Then you must *trust* children to go to the activity they need at that time to feed their emerging skills. You will find children who, left to their own devices, will choose to play in the block corner, or the dress-up corner, or paint at the easel again and again for weeks at a stretch. That tells you that these activities are satisfying some essential learning need in the child. As a teacher, you can add variety to these activities, bringing in different props, varying the material slightly, and playing with the children from time to time, expanding on their play and helping them build upon their ideas.

Each Child is Unique

Each chapter will describe, in general terms, what you can expect of "typical" children of various ages, what their capabilities, understandings and interests are. Please be aware that there is wide variation in the abilities and behaviors of "normal" children. Do not be alarmed if a particular child does not match a description exactly. Also remember that premature babies are often more in line with their regular due date than their actual age since birth. Although the rate of development varies from child to child, the "pattern" or "order" in which they learn skills and develop characteristics is quite consistent.

It's a good idea to read the chapters before and after the age group you are working with as well as that particular chapter. Some children may be advanced in physical skills and behind in language, or the other way around. It is always good to know where the child is coming from and where he is headed when looking at the current level of development. In child care situations, children are rarely grouped the way the chapters are divided in this book. There are often three-and-a-half-year-olds and young fours in the same group, for instance. Remember that growth is a continuum. A child doesn't suddenly stop being "two" and start being "three" on her third birthday.

This book is not meant to be used as a developmental checklist; rather, it is intended to give the reader an understanding and appreciation of the different stages of development. Specific ages are not given for the emergence of specific skills. I will not tell you, for instance, that by the time the child is four she should know the following things, and then go about listing them. Each child is different. The rate of development in various areas, motor, social, language, etc., may be uneven, with a child seeming to spurt ahead in one area while neglecting the others. It all evens out over time. Don't compare children to each other. Just respect the integrity of each individual child and trust him to develop at the pace that is just right for him. Look at the quality of the skill, rather than the age at which it is achieved.

If you have a concern about a child's development, make careful notes as to why you feel there is a problem. Confer with other professionals before alarming a parent with your suspicions. There are developmental screening tests child development specialists can use to assess the child. Early intervention can make big differences in the child's development. If you work with special needs children it's important to teach to their developmental level. However it is not as simple as that. A six-year-old child who is at a two-year-old cognitive developmental level may be at a different level physically. Work closely with parents and therapists to create a program that is just right for that child.

Another thing that makes each child unique is his temperament. Some children are shy or slightly fearful or cautious in new situations. They warm up slowly and may prefer watching other children play for a long time before they try an activity themselves. These children often spend much of their time hanging onto your leg. They may take a long time to adjust to a new child care situation. Other children burst right in, seeming to grab onto all new experiences with gusto, often throwing caution to the winds. Keeping these children safe is often a challenge! They may be impulsive and quick to squabble with other children, but often very creative as well. These children demand the lion's share of your attention. The majority of children are flexible and could be thought of as "easy." As long as they're feeling okay and safe, they are fairly good at finding something interesting to do, working out differences with other children and enjoying all you have to offer. The danger is that your attention will be diverted by other children and you will focus less on these undemanding children. Be sure to spend some one-on-one time with them whenever you can so they feel the warmth of your interest.

Don't Hurry Children

This is not a "curriculum book." The specific ideas and activities included are meant to give you an example of the type of activity that will promote the skill being discussed. They should be used as starting points to develop your own variations. You will quickly learn to simplify or add difficulty to an activity or toy. Are there too many words in the book? Turn the pages and simply tell the story, rather than reading it, adjusting the vocabulary to the level of the children in front of you. Is the puzzle too simple? Ask the child to try to put it together with eyes closed. Don't hesitate to end an activity that doesn't hold children's attention. Stay flexible.

It is also not the purpose of this book to have you "teach" skills at an earlier age. That would be like trying to teach children to get taller! And even if you could, why bother? Earlier is not better. Children grow according to their own inner timetable. However, although you cannot speed up a child's natural timetable for development, if children are not given adequate experiences, nutrition, health care and love, their development can be slowed down, and in some instances, permanently impaired.

It is hoped that you will become a "defender of childhood" and a child's right to play and live fully in the moment. The best way to prepare a child for the next stage is to let him live fully in the present stage. Enrich. Let the child take the lead. By understanding what to expect of the children in your care and respecting their innate drive to learn and develop, you can plan your program to present just the right challenge for children to allow them to learn at their optimum rate. That allows children to develop their potential. Stay tuned-in to your children, and enjoy them for the unique individuals that they are!

BRAIN DEVELOPMENT RESEARCH: WHAT IT TELLS US

Early childhood educators and sensitive parents have long known that the early years in a child's life are critically important. The quality of the child's experience during the first five years has an impact on virtually everything in the individual's development and ultimate success in life. In recent years the scientific community has offered "proof" – actual pictures of the child's brain made available with such technology as MRI (magnetic resonance imaging) and PET (positron emission tomography) scans.

The early years are extremely important in shaping the brain. It is a combination of experiences and genetics that determines an individual's capabilities.

By the time we are adults the brain has more than 100 billion brain cells called *neurons,* each reaching out to thousands of others so that all told, the brain has more than 100 trillion connections called *synapses.* That sounds like a whole lot, and it certainly is, but a one-year-old's brain has many times more! A baby is born prepared for any eventuality. The brain could grow in any direction, depending on the circumstances it encounters.

Just like someone who has over-packed for a long trip and gets tired of hauling around excess baggage, as a child develops, the unused synapses get discarded until at about age 12 the brain has pretty much the shape and pattern it will retain throughout life. For our traveler, what gets retained and what gets cast off depends on what gets used. Likewise for the young child's brain, the neurons and synapses that get used are the ones that are strengthened, and the unused pathways die off. The synapse pruning described above happens as a result of what the child experiences through his senses – what he sees, touches, smells, tastes and hears.

A child's genetic potential – the amount of brain cells she has to work with – needs support from the environment – the experiences she is offered. If she were kept in a white room in her early years and offered little stimulation, her intelligence would not develop.

Therefore: We should expose children to a wide variety of enriching experiences.

Emotions are important in shaping the brain. Early experiences significantly influence social and emotional brain functions, and a child's emotional states influence his ability to learn. Prolonged stress in infancy alters brain structure, giving people a predisposition to depression or aggression later in life.

Negative stresses, such as fear or anger, inhibit learning. Have you ever tried to learn something, or even pay attention, when you were frightened, frustrated, angry, or depressed? Have you ever tried to teach something to a crying child? Negative stresses release the brain chemical cortisol. When cortisol washes over the brain synapses they become unreceptive to stimulation. The "door" slams shut. Cortisol increases vigilance and attention to threat, and decreases attention to other things. (If you are frightened, you cannot focus on what people are saying.) When this is repeated and sustained over a long period of time, all those unused synapses die off from lack of use. Early intervention is critical when we know that infants and young children are in continuing stress.

What stresses a baby? Pain and not having needs met – such as in cases of neglect, abuse, chaos and lack of a consistent, loving caregiver. Poverty is a stressor. Of course, an infant doesn't care how much is in the bank account, but poverty and its complicating factors can so stress the parents that they are unable to respond to the needs of the baby.

On the other hand, positive stresses – joy, laughter, excited engagement – release serotonin, another brain chemical that establishes the "rest and digest" state of mind. That's when synapses are receptive to stimulation and learning can take place. Remember your favorite class in high school – the teacher you loved. The one who made you laugh, made you feel valued and respected, and shared her personal passion for the subject was the one you learned the most from. It has been found that laughter engages the brain in ways which alert and refresh our minds.

Since babies don't talk, emotional expressions, such as crying, coos and gurgles are the language of early relationships. Warm, responsive care seems to have a biologically protective function, helping children weather ordinary stresses. Love protects.

Therefore: We should provide young children with warm, stable relationships with caregivers who can accurately read and reflect their emotional state. We should involve excitement, joy, laughter and suspense in learning. Learning something with a loved one, or in a supportive circle of friends, makes it easy to take risks and experiment.

It's important to talk to children. Babies who are talked to in meaningful, responsive ways have a larger vocabulary at age two than babies who have had only minimal verbal stimulation. But it must be real, language about what is happening right now, right in front of the child. Recorded words, TV, and radio language do not benefit infants at all. There is no sensory connection – no meaning. A great deal of the child's vocabulary is acquired by age three. Even when a child is very young and doesn't understand the words, just hearing words builds up the ability of the brain to absorb more words.

Therefore: Be a "play by play announcer" describing what the child is doing and looking at. Also, provide lots of interesting experiences because they are vital in helping a child build vocabulary. The more a child uses his senses to explore the world around him, the more experiences he has to communicate about.

It's important to read to children. Studies have shown that children who are read to as preschoolers learn to read more easily than children who have not been exposed to books. But we know now that infants and toddlers also benefit greatly from being read to. Reading books is another way of talking to the child. Both the adult and the child are paying attention to one thing and screening out the rest of the things in the room. There is also the emotional connection. Snuggled warmly onto a lap, the child quickly gains the feeling that reading is a very pleasant thing to do. Gradually, children learn that books are a source of information and entertainment, and they start to see relationships between real life things and happenings and what they can find on the pages. They also figure out that those little black squiggles represent sounds.

Therefore: We should read often to children in warm, pleasant, informal ways, and develop a collection of high quality children's books. Some books are better than others. "Good literature" for young children is in books which have beautiful, clear illustrations and rich language with rhythm and resonances. Early exposure to the wonders available in the public library can also greatly increase children's interest in reading.

It's important to expose children to music. Singing to a baby is yet another way of talking to him. While sharing that aspect of your culture, you are also exposing the child to rhythms, intonations and words. Music also exposes children to cognitive concepts like sequences and repeated patterns.

Therefore: We should expose children to many kinds of music, including classical music, and actively involve children with the music. Encourage children to move to the music. Put a baby on your hip to dance and feel it. Enjoy the rhythms together. And of course, sing! Singing is language, cultural connections, and emotions all rolled into one.

Touch stimulates brain growth. New practices show that babies born prematurely, and at risk developmentally and medically, benefit greatly from touching and massage. It even enhances brain development when newborns are massaged, and premature babies gain weight more rapidly when parents massage them. The act of massaging their babies also helps parents develop that strong, instinctive bond that is so nurturing and protective to infants. Babies love to be cuddled and held close, and settle down when they are stroked, rocked, and gently bounced.

Therefore: We should build physical connections with children – lots of hugs, encouraging pats on the back, welcoming laps – warm, appropriate physical interactions with children.

Children need "hands-on" activities. One scientific study gives us a good parallel. William Greenough, a neuroscientist working at the University of Illinois, created a wonderful "play room" for laboratory rats, giving them many toys, colors and patterns, ramps, and all kinds of things that the rats could have fun with. He put several rats in that enriched environment to live and play to their hearts' content. In the middle of that space he placed another group of rats in a cage with no toys or things to do. They could spend their days watching all the other rats play. Then they examined the brains of both sets of rats. Guess what! The players had much bigger brains than the watchers. Repetition is also a critical factor in solidifying brain structure. It's what gets used over and over again that stays. "Practice makes permanent."

Therefore: Children should have a rich environment with a variety of experiences – hands-on experiences – and not be parked in front of a television set, passive for hours on end.

Children need to be physically active. Children who move and use their muscles have better cognitive development. Every preschool teacher knows that children need to be active in the classroom. More and more elementary school teachers are incorporating this into their teaching as well.

One thing we must be aware of is not keeping babies in devices that restrict their movement and exploration such as infant seats, bounce chairs, slings, back packs, swings, walkers, sitting support rings and high chairs. These things may have their function in keeping babies safe momentarily when the adult cannot be right at hand, but their use must be limited. Infants need to be free to use their muscles in order to learn and develop in optimal ways. If children are confined too much it can have detrimental effects on their curiosity and problem-solving abilities. Child care settings sometimes overuse these pieces of equipment. Do what you can to build awareness.

Therefore: We should think of ways to involve movement and physical activity into almost every activity we offer children and not expect that children be immobile and passive.

Good nutrition is critical for healthy development of the brain. The brain is, after all, physical tissue. The mother's prenatal nutrition is very important, as is what the child gets to eat when she is growing up. If a child is malnourished the brain diminishes right along with the body. Protein and water seem especially important, along with all the other nutrients.

Therefore: Offer nutritious meals and snacks and lots of water throughout the day, and raise parents' awareness of the importance of good nutrition, and of the resources available to them in the community.

There are critical periods for learning certain things.

The brain is "ripe" to learn certain things at particular points in the child's development. If the child is not exposed to the proper experiences during that time which foster that particular type of learning, it will be much more difficult later on.

Language. We have been surrounded by the evidence forever. It is most obvious in the area of language learning and acquiring a second language. In this country made up of people of diverse origins, we have ample evidence that people who immigrate here and try to learn English as adults almost never learn to speak without an accent. On the other hand, children under twelve learn a language quickly and almost effortlessly just by being exposed to it, and almost always speak without an accent. The implication here is to introduce foreign languages in elementary school rather than in high school. Interestingly, if a child learns a language during early childhood and forgets it later because of lack of exposure, it will be easier to relearn that language when re-exposed to it at an older age. We have also heard accounts of children who were isolated in neglectful or abusive situations and not exposed to language, who could not learn to speak later in life.

Music. There are few virtuoso musicians who began to study their instruments as older adolescents or adults. Almost all of them took up the instrument in early or middle childhood. Evidently, it is not the number of years someone studies the instrument that counts so much as how old they were when they started learning. Exposing children to many rich experiences with music in the first three years increases their aptitude to learn music later.

Vision. If for some reason, such as congenital cataracts, a child is unable to see things for the first two years of life, the brain loses capacity for vision. It is, therefore, critical that early vision problems be detected and, if possible, corrected.

Attachment. The emotional development window is from birth to two years, and it is difficult to compensate for later. Many children adopted after the age of two who come from bad orphanages, or who have been bounced from one foster home to another, have attachment disorders that are very difficult to overcome and have an impact on their entire personality and ability to learn. But others may thrive if the right kind of love gets to them quickly enough. Two factors – the quality of the care they received as infants, and their basic temperament, influence the child's ability to develop. If they have bonded with a caregiver even once, it helps. "'Tis better to have loved and lost, then never to have loved at all," to quote Tennyson.

What if you miss the window?

All is not lost. Except for the vision piece, it is still possible to learn after the optimal sensitive period. Adults can learn a second language or how to play an instrument. It simply takes more effort.

Incorporate new information with what you know.

We must rely on our instincts and what we know about good, developmentally appropriate practices, and not allow people to go off the deep end in search of the "quick fix" – "Buy this toy, this curriculum, this video, this infant stimulation package and we will have a nation of smarter kids." Good, consistent parenting, surrounded by love, security, rich language, books, and real experiences are what children need most.

Parents already have everything they need to maximize their child's brain development. No expensive toys or complicated programs are necessary – just touch, talk, singing, objects to examine, things to taste, opportunities to explore in a safe environment and most of all, warm, responsive, protective love.

CHAPTER 1

Birth to Six Months

LUCKY IS THE PERSON who gets to spend time around these youngest children. You, more than anybody, see the miracle of a new life, a developing person. Although much of an infant's time is spent sleeping or being fed and diapered, there is still time to play, cuddle and enjoy learning about what it means to be alive.

The recent research in brain development informs us that a new baby's brain is very busy, growing more rapidly than at any other time of life. Virtually everything the child experiences influences the structure of her brain. However, the baby does not need lots of extra stimulation because everything is brand new – each shadow, each face, each texture.

The caregiver of infants needs to be a very warm and responsive person, and able to interpret a baby's cries and gurgles. The baby needs your body to cling to. You also need to be well organized, keeping track of feeding and sleeping needs, good at keeping written records, and confident and relaxed in communicating with parents. Your most important responsibility is to keep the infant safe and physically comfortable, and in a group care situation, this sometimes means protecting the baby from older, inquisitive children. Finally, you need to allow yourself to fall in love with the baby. From you, parents, and close family members, the baby is learning what it is to be a human being.

SOCIAL EMOTIONAL DEVELOPMENT

This is a time when a baby makes her first connections with people and begins to develop an awareness of being lovable in the responses she receives from others.

Issues of Emotional Development and Self-esteem

"Bonding" and developing "basic trust" are the closely related essentials for human emotional development that have their vital roots in early infancy.

Bonding

A "bond" is the instinctive strong attachment of human and animal babies to their mothers. It is these strong emotional feelings of attachment, which cause the adult to care for and protect the totally helpless infant, that allows the species to survive. The baby is an active player in the process, in the way she stares at the mother's face, nuzzles in to her neck, and coos with contentment, causing the adult to respond with pleasure. The instinctive bond to the mother comes first. This must be in place for the normal emotional development to take place. It is important to understand that this doesn't necessarily have to be the biological mother. In cases where the biological mother is not available because of sickness, death, emotional illness, adoption or some other cause, a primary caregiver or "mothering one," can provide this bond. This could be a father, grandparent or foster parent. This first human emotional attachment, though, is the starting point for all human relationships. Then the child can expand the circle to other human beings, at first just a few. As a child care provider you are providing a secondary bond. That's why it is important to minimize staff turnover in an infant program, so that the child is cared for by one or two loving, caring, familiar adults. Most programs now are assigning each infant new to the program a primary caregiver – one adult who develops an especially close relationship with the child and the child's parents. Do reassure the parent that the close bond you establish with the child fosters the child's emotional development and will never replace the primary bond the child has with the parents.

Basic Trust

"Basic trust" develops as the child learns that her needs will be met. She learns this by a rhythm of distress and relief. The child feels the distress of hunger and cries. The mother or caregiver hears the cry, comes and picks up the baby and feeds her. The distress is relieved. This pattern is repeated and consistent. When a child learns she can trust mother/caregiver to relieve her distress, the trust grows into a feeling of security, and later confidence to try new things.

The concept of basic trust is one good reason, among many others, that babies should be on a demand schedule rather than a schedule contrived for the convenience of adults. The child should sleep, be fed, diapered, cuddled and played with according to the child's own inner schedule. The caregiver must tune-in to the baby's signals and know the baby well enough to make accurate guesses about what the child needs so she can respond appropriately.

Touch

Babies thrive on being touched. While full infant massage might best be left to parents in the home setting, infants in your care will enjoy and be soothed by gentle stroking, such as putting baby lotion on their arms and legs.

Relationships with Other People

The newborn baby is usually pretty sober when awake and not crying. However, she will stare intently at a human face around eight to twelve inches from her eyes, and will turn her head toward voices. She is definitely interested in people.

Newborns and young infants seem to show an instinctive empathy for others. This is most noticeable when one baby starts crying and soon all the others have joined in. Experienced caregivers report that singing to the children seems to help stop this group wailing. It sets up some different vibrations for the babies to listen to.

Feeding

It is not by mistake that this topic is put under social development rather than physical development. It involves another person, and the child communicates needs. Getting fed is the most important thing that happens in a baby's day, especially from the baby's point of view. Not only is she getting nourishment, she is absorbing all the nurturing – the holding and cuddling and body contact – and developing some basic attitudes about food, and bodies. A young baby should always be held when fed, and enough time allowed so the caregiver can be relaxed and at ease.

Some new babies experience a lot of gastric distress. A colic condition can last up to three months. Introducing new foods can also cause some distress. For this reason, new food should always be introduced by parents at home, preferably on a weekend, to see how the child tolerates it.

Communicate closely with parents about what the baby should have to eat and drink. (Of course, these decisions are made by parents in conjunction with their health care providers.) Most babies quickly establish a routine of regular intervals when they are hungry. Knowing each baby's routine will help you plan your day, but remember to listen to the child's signals rather than just watching the clock. All child care situations for infants should have specific procedures for keeping written records of when, what and how much an infant ate.

Smiling

It is at around six weeks of age that the child develops that irresistible social smile that warms the heart of any adult who is the lucky recipient. This is a critical step in the bonding process in which the baby captures any loving adult in the vicinity. A baby will usually smile at almost any face that appears about one foot

away from her eyes, even a doll or teddy bear; however, they smile longest and strongest for the parent. At about three months comes that wonderful belly-laugh and joyful excitement. The infant genuinely enjoys social contact with familiar people. Find many ways to play and interact with each other.

"Ah-Boo!"

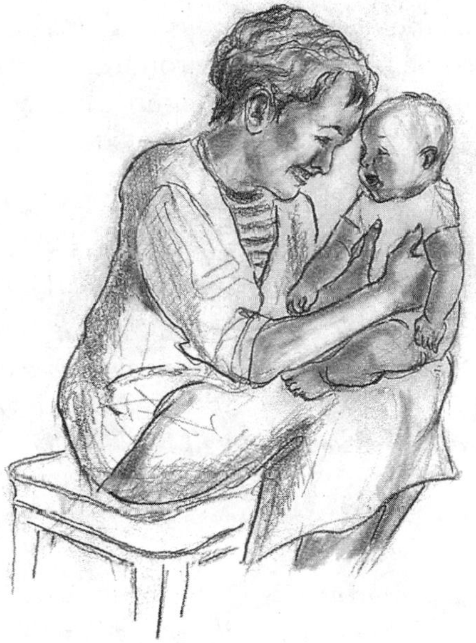

This is the type of game that people have been playing with babies since time began. Place the child on your lap in front of you. Smile and say, "Ah-boo" as you lean toward the baby and gently bump your forehead to the baby's. Repeat this as long as the activity seems enjoyable to the baby.

Take advantage of your routine times – diapering, feeding, dressing, etc. – for easy social interactions like this. Take your time, when you can, and enjoy these precious one-to-one moments.

Visual Development

A baby's social development is affected by her growing ability to see faces, colors and movement. The vision of a newborn is much sharper than once thought. The child will look into the eyes of the person holding her. A new baby will also stare at a drawing of the upper half of a human face when it is placed nearby. However, real faces are much more interesting than drawings of faces and it is not necessary to post face drawings in the infant environment.

Babies are also visually attracted to bright colors, sharp contrasts and patterns such as attractive quilt patterns. They are also interested in things that move and can follow them with their eyes. That is one reason mobiles that jiggle or rotate are interesting. Since babies should not be left in cribs when they are awake in a child care situation, it is not necessary to put mobiles or crib toys in the crib. However, you might want to hang some in the play environment where a baby could see it easily when lying on her back. (Make sure the mobile is interesting when viewed from underneath – the baby's position.)

Tracking

Place the baby on her back on the floor. Hold a bright object about twelve inches over her head and jiggle it to get her attention. Then move the object from side to side slowly, and allow the baby to follow the object with her eyes. She may show excitement and move her arms and legs. How long will this keep her interest?

Mirror

Attach an unbreakable mirror to the wall sideways at floor level. An older baby who can hold her head up will be entertained lying on her stomach in front of the mirror. A low mirror will remain interesting to infants at all stages.

When the child is about six weeks old she becomes skillful at following objects with her eyes, and can focus on all distances. Hold the baby upright on your shoulder so she can look around the room, or place her on your lap, facing outward, while you are sitting on the floor in the play area. She will enjoy watching the other children at play.

Typical Behavior Issues

It is not appropriate to talk about "discipline" concerning young babies. Infants in their first year do not willfully misbehave to vex adults. They do not have the experience or mental systems to understand cause and effect relationships and what makes others mad. It is when adults misunderstand this that the most tragic instances of abuse of infants occur. Babies cry because of some physical distress, pain or fear, not to annoy.

Crying

Crying is an infant's first way of communicating with you and letting you know she needs something – that something is making her uncomfortable. People caring for infants should make every effort to pick up crying babies promptly and try to comfort them. In generations past there was the idea that picking up babies could "spoil" them and they should be left to "cry it out" so that they do not become demanding as they grow older. This notion has been proven untrue. In fact, babies who are picked up promptly and cared for in a very responsive way turn out to be more content and compliant in the second half of their first year, and later toddlerhood. Also, having an adult who responds dependably to a baby's distress is a direct predictor of a child having positive social relationships with other children later on. It's as though they have to experience kindness to give it out later.

This is one good reason for low staff/child ratios in infant programs. If you cannot get right to a crying baby because you are busy with another child, still offer reassurance. Touch and pat the child if you can, and at least give verbal assurance. "Yes, Nathan, I hear you. I know you are hungry. I'll come and get you in a minute." Your tone of voice can be reassuring.

It is instinctively distressing to adults to hear a crying baby. Often a baby's cry will be relieved by feeding or diapering. But at times this is not enough. Sometimes the caregiver will have fed, "burped," and diapered a baby, and determined that the child is not feverish or otherwise ill, and the child will still cry. It could be a bellyache or some other internal tension. Other ways to comfort the new baby are walking with the baby, rocking, singing, and giving the child a pacifier. Interestingly, babies often seem to respond best to fast, little rocks – about 60 beats per minute. Perhaps it is because this approximates the mother's heart beat. Ask the parents how they comfort the baby at home and try to duplicate that process. There might be a special position a baby prefers. Babies should be held close and comforted, even if they continue to cry. Your mere presence is offering sympathy.

Sucking

Sucking is a strong need for babies under a year, and especially for newborns. If a child is fortunate enough to locate her own thumb, fingers or fist to suck on, by all means allow it. A pacifier can bring welcome comfort to a fretful baby, and is not considered harmful by doctors, if you keep it clean.

GROSS MOTOR DEVELOPMENT

Head Control and Mobility

Newborns cannot lift their heads. Always provide head support when you lift or hold a new baby. At about six or eight weeks the baby might be able to hold her head up when held upright. Lying on her back, she can move her head from side to side, and is often seen with knees bent and both hands brought to the middle of her chest. When you place her on her stomach, her head will be to one side. Although the baby cannot roll over or move around, some babies, when angry, manage to propel their bodies the entire length of the crib by repeatedly digging their feet into the mattress surface and thrusting out with their legs. That is why a bumper pad placed around the edges of the crib is a good idea.

Gradually, the infant learns to stretch out her limbs and lie flat on her back, able to look above her as well as to the side, and wave her arms and legs around.

Head and Torso Control

It is at around six weeks of age that a baby first starts to lift her head and look around when placed on her stomach. By three months she's getting pretty good at it and can raise her chest, supported by her arms. At about three or four months the baby is getting more torso control and may even roll over before long.

Rolling Over

You do not need to motivate a baby to roll over. When she is ready, she will do it. The only thing that is necessary is freedom, on the floor. Place interesting objects near the baby and she will begin reaching for them, twisting and turning and eventually rolling over from tummy to back and from back to tummy.

Kicking

If you place something at the bottom of the feet of a baby of six or eight weeks of age, she is likely to kick out against it. Held upright with feet against the floor, the baby may thrust out legs against the floor. When the baby is three to six months old she will greatly enjoy making powerful leg thrusts when lying on her back.

> *Foot Gong*
>
> *Try holding a cookie sheet at the feet of a three-month-old for her to bang her feet against.*

Moving Around

Although it is rare for infants to crawl with tummies off the ground before the age of six months, they can find many other ways to move across space. The twisting, stretching and rolling lead to "scootching" of some sort or other, propelling themselves by thrusting legs, or hauling themselves along with their arms.

It is important that infants not be confined in devices that restrict movement for long periods of time, such as infant seats, bounce chairs, slings, padded "sitting rings." The child needs active practice, using and strengthening muscles, and the freedom to move. Place the child on a clean blanket or sheet on the floor when she is awake so she can practice twisting and moving her body. You do not need to contrive exercises for babies. They are naturally motivated to move – just give them the opportunity.

FINE MOTOR DEVELOPMENT

Fists

A new baby's hands are closed in tight fists. If you pry the fingers open and put your finger across the palm of her hand, the baby's fingers will close tightly around your finger. This is why new babies can hold onto a rattle. The rattle will not have any meaning for the baby though, and she may even hit herself in the face with it, so it's not a good idea to have a newborn hold a rattle just because she can.

Discovering Hands

At about six weeks the baby's hands will relax more and start to open. It is at this stage when the child is lying on her back that she will suddenly notice her hands moving across her field of vision. What a fascinating discovery! The child will spend a lot of time staring at her hands, and discover that she has some control over those funny moving things!

Hand Mitts

Make some little "mitts" from baby socks by cutting holes in them for fingers to stick out of. Use permanent markers to draw little faces on them. These make hands even more interesting to look at.

Batting

When the child is two or three months old she may start swiping or batting at interesting objects dangled overhead. At first these gestures will be very erratic and jerky. This is the time to take flimsy mobiles out of cribs and replace them (at home) with sturdy "crib gyms" designed for children to grab and pull on. Make sure the objects are securely attached.

Target Practice

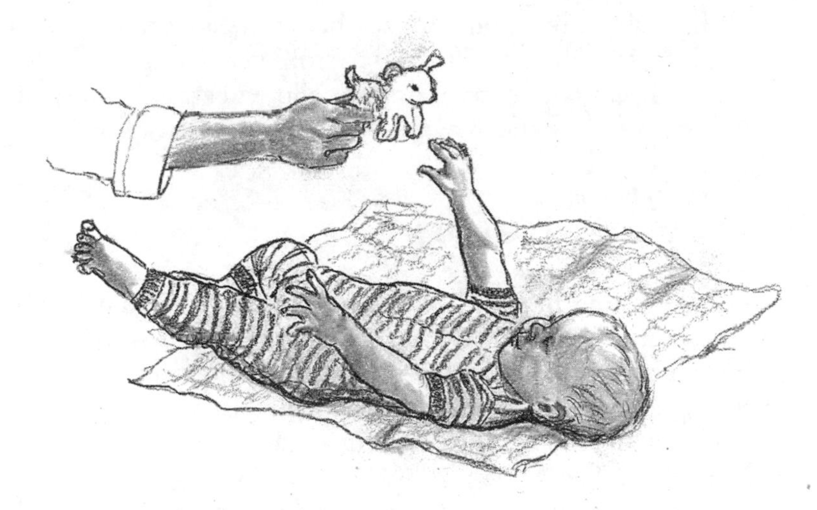

Hold a toy that makes an interesting noise over the child's head when the child is lying on the floor. Jiggle it to get the child to bat at it. (The child will also enjoy kicking at this.)

Grasping

At four months, when an object is placed in a child's hand, she is likely to look at it and bring it to her mouth to be gummed. Also, she might actually succeed in grabbing something. It won't be easy though. She is not yet good at opening her hand before she makes contact with the object, and her aim is fairly random. This is a good time to offer the child a rattle. She will enjoy the cause and effect of making a noise, and learn how to let go of it and pick it up again. Once a child can pick something up, it goes right to the mouth for further exploration, so make sure things are safe and too large to choke on.

When a child succeeds in grasping or hitting something and making it move, she is gaining a sense of personal power – she can make things happen in the world. It is quite exciting to the baby and she will seek more and more opportunities.

Look for all kinds of toys and objects which the child can pick up and manipulate in different ways. Also keep an eye out for interesting textures on objects for the child to finger.

Discovering Feet

Not long after the child discovers her hands, she discovers her feet! Wow! When the baby is lying on her back her knees are often bent with her feet sticking straight up. What interesting visual targets they make as they move around up there. Soon the child will grasp her feet and hang on and enjoy feeling the dynamics of her own body.

LANGUAGE DEVELOPMENT

Of course, young babies do not produce or understand words, but language is much more than words. Long before a baby can understand and produce words, she will understand intonations. Just as you, hearing strangers speaking a foreign language, know if they are angry, frightened or in love by the tone of their speech, a baby can sense your emotional state and will reflect that.

Crying is a baby's first form of verbal communication. What she is finding out is that when she produces noises, she'll get some action. That is language. She is seeing the beginnings of language as a means to an end – getting her needs met.

After about two months she will also enjoy gurgling and making noises with her saliva. You'll hear all kinds of guttural and vowel sounds and the intonation or melody of language will gradually become apparent in the child's jabbering and squeals of delight. Simple consonant sounds get added as time goes on. While the baby makes random sounds like this, she is learning what mouth positions create which sounds, and these become more and more refined as time goes on. It's great fun to hear a baby talking to herself practicing the sounds she has heard and learning what she can do with her mouth.

Infants are born with the ability to learn any language they are exposed to, and have the capabilities to produce all language sounds. Gradually, the brain prunes the language sounds the child is able to differentiate and reproduce, according to the sounds the child hears from people close to her. By the way, it does no harm for infants to hear more than one language, as can happen when a caregiver speaks a different language from the child's parents, or the two parents speak different languages at home. In fact, it could be considered a gift. Babies have an amazing ability to absorb language – their brains are extremely flexible. The language sounds the child hears in the first year of life are the ones that will become natural and permanent to the child. But keep in mind that the language sounds must come from real human beings, not television, radio or tapes, to have this benefit.

By all means, talk to babies. You are giving her a feel for language, and by talking to the baby, you are actually strengthening the pathways in the brain that allow the child to learn language. If you describe what you are doing and what the child sees going on, you are helping her to gradually attach meaning to words. Not surprisingly, research shows that children who are talked to a lot become more talkative themselves, and develop a larger vocabulary at an earlier age. Also keep in mind that talking is a two-way street. Have conversations with the baby, taking turns.

Circles of Talk

Place the baby on a clean blanket on the floor, on her back. Lean over her and make eye contact. Talk to her in sweet, soothing tones – any nonsense that comes to mind. Pause and see if the child makes eye contact, smiles and makes noises back to you. Does she pause and wait for you to take a turn? Imitate the child's noises. See how many of these "circles" or turns you can make happen with her. When you respond to her in this way, you are giving her a feeling of power.

Early Literacy

Yes, it is appropriate to think about pre-reading, or early literacy activities, even with the youngest infants. Just about everything a child experiences relates to later learning to read. It helps to be conscious of how this happens. The child is busy getting body rhythms regulated and sensory systems such as vision and hearing coordinated so she can attend – learn to pay attention to one thing – certainly a skill necessary for reading. Explorations of objects give infants information about size, shape and position, all necessary to making sense of those marks on a page. When you talk to a baby you are preparing her brain for learning language patterns. Likewise, singing reinforces patterns of intonation, rhythm and speech.

Books

And, yes, you should be reading books to infants. Reading a book to a baby is one way of talking to the child. When the child is alert and calm, place her on your lap and hold a bright book where you can both see it comfortably. The child is learning to focus on patterns, and hears language coming from you. She hears you say something about each picture as you point to it. You will later see her imitate this behavior. She is paying attention to the book in front of her, learning to screen out other things in the room. She learns to explore the book as an interesting object, enjoying the mechanics of turning the pages. Perhaps most important, it is a warm, pleasant experience and the child will associate reading with emotional closeness. Good books for infants have bright colors and uncomplicated illustrations or photographs of things the child might see in her environment. Books should also be sturdy enough not to tear or fall apart when an infant grasps them, mouths them, and experiments with the pages.

COGNITIVE DEVELOPMENT

Cognitive development and thinking skills have a sensory base. The child has to absorb much information using all her senses in order to start abstract thinking later on and form mental images of things not right in front of her. It's fascinating to watch this little scientist on a new planet. The new infant is busy using all of her senses to investigate this world.

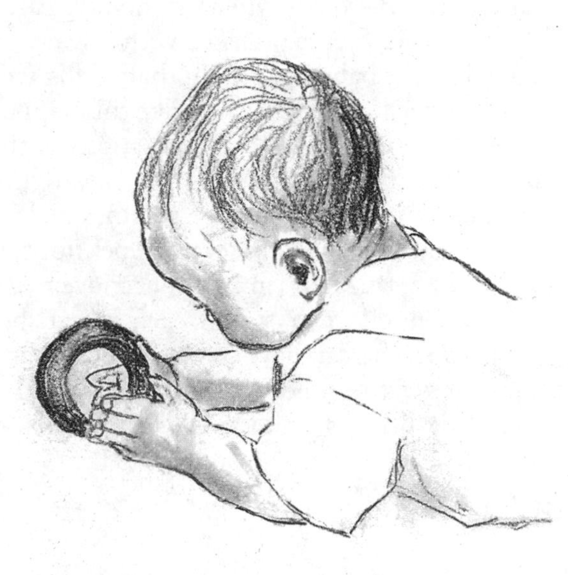

Object Hunger

Once an infant can grasp things, "object hunger" kicks in. The child is "hungry" for objects, and is driven to pick up and examine everything she sees. First it goes into the mouth for the most sensitive sensory examination (therefore, make sure any object within reach of a baby is too large to choke on and safe to mouth). She will likely turn the object over, bang it on the floor, drop it, pick it up again, put it back in her mouth, etc. She is gaining information about the properties of physical objects. Expect much ongoing exploration over the next year and a half.

Lack of Object Permanence

A baby cannot keep a mental image of an object she cannot see. "Out of sight, out of mind." For instance, it is typical for a six-month-old to grab at the glasses of someone holding her. All you have to do is take them off and put them out of sight, even in a pocket where she can still reach them. Even if you do this right in front of the child, she will forget about them and not reach for them. Try this with other objects, like an attractive toy. In a couple months it will be different and the child will go after the desired object.

Cause and Effect

It's an exciting discovery when the infant learns she can make something happen. It's her first experience with power. The earliest realization of this is when the baby figures out that crying will make someone appear. Not long afterwards, something like this happens: the infant, randomly kicking in her crib, feeling the sensations of the bouncing bed, notices that a crib mobile jiggles. She stops to watch it. Eventually the mobile stops and, out of boredom, she resumes kicking. Then she notices the mobile jiggling again. After several repetitions, it occurs to the child that she is making this happen with her movements. Now begins the long and persistent effort to explore each object she encounters to see what kind of effect she can have on it. Objects that make a noise get special interest. Once the child can grasp things and starts to explore objects, it is the ideal time to offer rattles and "shake-shake toys" of all types.

MUSIC

Babies enjoy music from the very beginning. Lullabies have been used since the beginning of time to comfort babies. All cultures have lullabies. Live singing while being held is a wonderful gift for a baby. The child feels the vibrations of your body as she hears the sounds. She is learning part of the human repertoire. It doesn't matter at all, of course, whether you can hold a tune or not. Also hold the baby close to you and dance to the music, allowing her to feel the rhythm.

Play all kinds of music for the children, except for loud rock music. Classical music is especially good, but lively, rhythmic dance music, folk music and music from the children's home cultures are great as well. Generally, play music by plan and listen to it consciously with children rather than having endless background music which soon gets screened out.

HOW THEY PLAY

Young babies need play time when they are fed, comfortable, and alert. The youngest infants' play involves learning how to use this body they've been issued, and then examining the wonderful world of objects available to them. The adult's role in the child's play is to create a safe environment, put things in it that the child can use to expand on skills she already has, or is just learning, and to know when to interact and when to step back and let the child experiment on her own.

Place the baby in the play area and be close by for supervision and for social interaction. Be sensitive not to interrupt a baby when she is playing with something or is fascinated with exploring a new object. Also be conscious of fatigue on the part of the baby. They can tolerate only so much stimulation. After you have dangled an object for a baby to look at or swipe at for a few minutes, for instance, you may notice the baby look away or fuss. Each child will have a different attention span for all play activities, so remain sensitive to their signals.

The Play Environment

An environment for young, non-mobile infants should include a clean, carpeted floor space where an adult can sprawl out comfortably with a baby. Again the caution – do not restrict the child by keeping her in infant seats, bounce chairs, etc. She should have the freedom to move and use her muscles. If cleanliness is a concern, you can spread a clean bed sheet on the floor and tuck it under the edges of an area rug, or simply put a clean baby blanket on the floor. Another rule of thumb is never to put babies in a position they cannot achieve by themselves. For instance don't place a baby in a sitting position when she cannot sit up unsupported.

Some state child care licensing regulations require the presence of a playpen, not for confining babies, but for protecting them. A young infant can be placed inside a playpen for a few minutes while the adult cannot be right there next to her, and be relatively safe from the curious advances of older infants and toddlers. There are also wonderful manufactured "nests" of vinyl-covered foam that allow you to separate the youngest babies from older ones. You can also create an enclosed space with other things such as bolsters and cushions and small room dividers.

Create interesting things to look at. Pictures and patterns can be attached to vertical surfaces at floor level. Attach transparent colored plastic to windows for the light to shine through. Bottles filled with colored water on a high windowsill will create beautiful color patterns on the floor and walls.

Have a wide assortment of objects for babies to hold and examine and put in their mouths. Naturally, be careful that they are safe and the child could not choke on them, and they can be easily washed and kept clean. In addition to standard baby toys, look for objects that move in interesting ways such as plastic soft drink bottles, balls and plastic eggs. Large, bright inflatable plastic beach toys are appealing. If you leave them soft, under-inflated, they are easier for a child to grasp. Also good are objects with interesting surfaces, indentations and textures such as teddy bears, plastic soap holders, measuring spoons connected with a ring, plastic ice cube trays and bright cloth napkins. Books suitable for babies to handle should also be in the environment, both published and homemade.

Going Outside

It can be very beneficial to bring young infants outside in mild weather. Spread a blanket in a shady spot and provide a few simple toys and you're all set. The infant will look at the moving shadows of the leaves, feel the breeze on her skin and hear the sounds of nature. You could hang a bright wind sock or pieces of colored plastic to make pretty patterns. Be there to supervise, of course. An infant could choke on natural objects such as stones, acorns or leaves. Protect young infants from older explorers. A large, expandable play fence is used by some. Also consider letting infants nap outside in a shady spot. You can bring cribs or carriages outside. The fresh air is very conducive to slumber.

SUMMARY

In caring for infants between birth and six months, concentrate not so much on "teaching" as on providing a warm, nurturing relationship and environment. Responsibilities fall into four major areas:

1. Responsive Care

The most important thing in the first six months of life is good, responsive, physical care of babies. Responsive means staying tuned-in to the baby's cues, picking up and comforting promptly, and allowing the baby to sleep, eat and be changed according to her own rhythms. Provide lots of holding, cuddling and loving attention.

Try to keep things as calm and as consistent as possible. One of a baby's main tasks is to learn to regulate herself – to fall into a comfortable rhythm of sleeping, eating, being awake.

2. Strong Relationship with Parents

The importance of working closely in a mutually respectful relationship with parents cannot be overstated. You are not a substitute parent. Instead, you are a parent support system. Earning a parent's "basic trust" is as important as gaining that from the infant. Do everything you can to strengthen the parent/child bond, helping the parent appreciate what a wonderful, unique individual their child is. Make an extra effort to have warm, supportive, face-to-face communications with the parents as well as good record keeping. Sometimes this will take an extra dose of understanding by you because parting with a baby is a very emotional and difficult thing to do.

3. Freedom to Explore

The child should have opportunities when awake to move, stretch, grasp, kick, roll and otherwise use her body and handle objects in a clean, safe environment.

4. Interaction Between Caregiver and Baby

Talk, sing and play, responding verbally to the sounds the infant makes. The muscles of the brain need to be exercised as well as those of the body.

CHAPTER 2

Six Months to One Year
The Mobile Infant

THIS IS A BABY who is really getting interesting. Up to now the child has been a cute little bundle whose needs centered mainly around cuddling, a lot of physical contact and good, responsive physical care in the management of feeding, diapering and sleeping routines. The older baby still needs all that, of course, but now we have a child who reaches, sits up, moves and vocalizes in a most engaging way. What an exciting age! It is the physical development that dominates everything. In this brief span of months the child moves from someone just able to scootch around the floor to someone who can walk and begin to explore the universe! The non-mobile baby becomes mobile.

SOCIAL EMOTIONAL DEVELOPMENT

Issues of Emotional Development and Self-esteem

The child between six and twelve months of age is typically pleasant and fun to be around, as long as he is feeling well, although this may change once the child becomes mobile and is no longer content to just sit and look. At the beginning of this stage the child is usually friendly to almost anyone and smiles easily. As with younger infants, these babies need very much to feel secure in the love of their caregivers. It is important for the caregiver to cuddle, hug and generally rejoice in the child. Caring for infants of any age must be a love affair.

Stranger Anxiety

Although not all children go through this, many babies who were formerly very open and accepting of new people, at about eight months of age become frightened of new faces. Children will develop attachments to certain people – members of the immediate family and their primary caregivers – and nobody else may come near!

The child's basic temperament influences his tolerance for new situations and strangers. It's true that children in group child care situations experience less stranger anxiety than children cared for at home because they are used to many people coming in and out of the environment. When a new child has trouble adjusting, it helps a great deal if the same caregiver receives the child from the parent every morning, and assumes primary responsibility for him during the day. The child must develop trust in one adult first before he can generalize his feeling of comfort to other people.

This may be a particularly difficult time for a child to enter child care and experience a major change in his life. It will simply take patience and gentle understanding on the part of the caregiver, as well as compassion for the pain the child's distress causes the parents. Eventually the child will develop trust in the caregiver and become attached to this new, familiar face.

When babies cry and cling to you in fear when strangers are around, allow the child the security of your lap. If the child feels safe, he may crawl down on his own and approach the new person.

Pride

The child is making such exciting progress in physical abilities during this period. Mastering a new physical skill is very exciting. The child's face will show it. "Wow...I did it!!!" It's important for the adults in the child's life to share in this joy and excitement. "Look at you! You're standing up! You did it!" A round of applause is not inappropriate.

The adult's endorsement will give the child encouragement to go on trying new things. Basking in the approval of important adults is vital to the development of the child's self-esteem, and later, psychological and intellectual development. Of course, this interest from adults is important all through childhood. Share in children's pride and excitement in their new accomplishments.

Relationships with Other People

A baby this age enjoys interactions with other people. He can enjoy prolonged play with a favorite adult and is inclined to giggle a lot. The give and take of social relationships and play are being learned. Get down on the floor and play with the baby. Play peek-a-boo and laugh at each other. Let the child crawl over you and in and out of your lap. Enjoy and encourage his sociability. Greet other people who come around with friendliness and openness while you are with the baby, providing a social model for the child.

Social Games

<u>*Hand It Over*</u>

With the child sitting in front of you, hand him an attractive object and say, "Here you are." Then reach out your open hand, palm up, smile, look expectant and say, "Please give it to me." The child will probably hand it back to you. If not, gently take it back. Then say, "Thank you!" Then reach out and hold the object toward the child and repeat, "Here you are." See if you can get the child to repeat this sequence back and forth several times.

Watching

It is common for a child close to one year old to stop all activity and just watch other children at play. The child is actually taking it all in, a kind of mental practice before later engaging in the activity himself. Sometimes simple looking is the most common activity other than sleeping at this age.

Baby Friendships

We know that infants have a genuine interest in other children. From the very beginning they love looking at faces, especially faces of children. Because of the growth of group infant care, it has become apparent that children also form friendships of a "baby sort." With special friends, children with whom they are familiar, they will make eye contact, and if able, sometimes move to be close to the other child. As they approach toddlerhood, they may even begin to imitate the actions of their friend.

Typical Behavior Issues

Setting Limits

It is an often a difficult time for adults when a baby starts to get around, reach for things and climb. Once the child can get around, even before he is walking, he enters the famous "into everything" stage of development. This is the time to "babyproof" the environment, putting away breakable objects. These very young children are impulsive. They don't think about the consequences before they do something. And they have an innate drive to pick up everything they see.

And then there is the physical development exploration – pulling up on everything, crawling in and behind things, climbing! It's wise to have an environment where much physical activity is allowable so you're not shouting, "No!" all the time, or worse, confining him in some sort of "baby trap" so he cannot move about. Remember that he has to use his body and practice new skills. If the child starts to climb on the table, take him down, and say, "Tables are not for climbing. Let's go over to the slide."

Rather than setting limits verbally, or by punishment, set limits physically, by placing barriers to keep children away from dangerous places like stairs, fireplaces, stoves and tippy furniture. Put fragile things away, out of sight. Otherwise, you are fighting nature. The child cannot stop himself at this point. And if you confine the child too much or constantly prohibit exploration, you risk dampening his curiosity. All this exploration has a genuine cognitive learning purpose.

Hurting Others

These infants know how to grab and pull at things. They are also eagerly exploring objects, finding out what kind of exciting effects they can cause. Another baby is simply a very interesting object to explore. Grabbing a handful of someone else's cheek, or pulling hair creates a very exciting effect...lots of noise! Some children will even start to bite at this age, for the same reasons. These behaviors are all in the realm of exploration and should not be treated as aggressive acts. Instead, stay close, anticipate and interrupt. If you see a child reaching for another, move close and help him touch gently. If he is already in the act and the other child is crying for help, move in, release his grasp, and use a concerned, empathetic tone of voice. "Oh no, you're hurting Peter. See, he's crying. Touch Peter gently, like this."

Touch the infant doing the hurting in a gentle way. Say, "Gentle." Then help him touch you, and then the other child, saying all the time, "Gentle." Even though the child doesn't understand your words, he understands your tone of voice. Don't shout or frighten the child, but show empathetic concern.

GROSS MOTOR DEVELOPMENT

So much progress in such a short time span! The baby has a strong need to practice each new skill over and over again. The drive to be vertical is incredibly strong. The world is just a whole lot more exciting from that position. So much of the child's efforts lead in this direction.

Rolling Over

Around the age of six months, sometimes earlier, sometimes later, the child will gain enough torso control to turn over from back to stomach and from stomach to back. It's really fun to watch the first few times the baby succeeds at this. There is an expression of startled surprise and amazed excitement on his face. And, of course, he wants to do it again!

There is no need to "teach" a child to roll over. It is one of those things he will learn to do by himself. All you have to do is provide him with the opportunity. When the child is awake, put him on a clean blanket on the floor, lying down on his back or stomach, perhaps with a few interesting objects around to reach for and handle.

Some babies enjoy rolling over so much that rolling becomes their prime means of getting from one place to another.

Creeping and Crawling

Crawling is defined as moving using the arms to pull the body along, with the abdomen on the floor.

Creeping is when the child moves on hands and knees with the abdomen above the floor.

At around six months, the baby may start to crawl or "scootch" across the floor in some way. The baby usually starts by trying to get at something just out of reach. Place the baby, lying down on his stomach, on a clean, carpeted floor with a number of interesting small toys in the area, some within reach, some just out of reach. By putting a few things out of reach, you will motivate the child to practice moving across a space.

The transition from crawling to creeping is fun to watch. The child will often rock back and forth on hands and knees without making progress, but enjoying the feeling. Some babies can't seem to get into forward gear at first, and mainly creep backwards. Occasionally, babies skip the creeping stage, going directly to pulling up and walking around holding onto things.

Make sure the baby has plenty of free floor time to gain experience crawling and creeping. They need the practice of making their arms and legs work together. Provide interesting surfaces to move over.

<u>Texture Trail</u>

Gather variously textured materials to spread across your floor for children to crawl across. Carpet samples, hemp door mats, rubber door mats, artificial turf door mats, and throw rugs can be lined up to make an interesting trail for the child to follow. These things can be gathered up and put away, to be put out in a different arrangement each day.

Sitting Up

Once the baby can roll over, sitting up is not far behind. It requires the ability to hold the head steady, and to have the torso control to maintain balance. Again, you don't need to teach a baby to sit up. He simply needs time on the floor, free of restraints, to experiment with all the different ways he can move.

Learning to sit up independently is a big step forward developmentally. There is often a burst in curiosity and movement. The child sees the world from a new perspective and can spot things across the room. When placed on the floor in a lying down position the child will often push himself up to a sitting position. With this new control of his posture, the child is itching to get at the rest of the world and come in contact with the enticing objects that are out of reach. So, when this milestone is reached it is a good time to recheck your environment for safety.

Pulling Up

Once the child can sit up and crawl it is not long before he starts to pull up to a standing position using any stationary object handy. Being able to stand up produces great pride of accomplishment. The child, once ready, will pull up on anything available, so make sure that furniture is stable. Also, be aware of hazards such as tablecloths or dangling appliance cords because the child will pull on them, and may cause things to fall down on him.

Cruising

"Cruising" is the term used when children walk along side stepping, holding on to furniture such as sofas, walls or low tables. See how you can arrange furniture and other stable objects to give children plenty of safe things to grab onto and walk around. You might even attach low railings to the wall about eighteen inches off the floor.

Standing Alone

Once the child is good at cruising, the next step is to stand alone. Those sturdy little legs are squarely under the child in a wide stance, and balance is still wobbly. A child will usually stand alone when he is within reach of some stable object to grab onto for security. Later he will get up to a standing position from a sitting position, without the aid of something to pull up on.

Walking

When children take their first step varies widely. Some are ready to go as early as nine months. Others don't venture out until they are as old as fourteen months. Some children seem to take off running. Others, while they may take an independent step now and then, are much more cautious and make the transition to walking independently gradually. In any case, what a daring accomplishment! With his newfound skill, this baby will need constant watching. It is the age of falling down, running into things and pulling on anything within reach. It's interesting that new walkers like to carry something in each hand, almost as if they are still holding on for security. In spite of numerous minor injuries that seem to go with the age, the drive to walk is so strong that the child will get up and do it again and again until he drops from exhaustion.

Open spaces with soft carpeted surfaces are desirable for children learning to walk. Try to stay in control of clutter. Although there will always be toys on the floor, try to minimize the number of things to stumble over.

Walking leads to running...and running away. The lure of the open road is irresistible! You will often see a child this age take off into a large open space like a hall or airport or restaurant, with a parent in hot pursuit. There is an invisible rubber band that eventually pulls the child back to the parent, but for some children this rubber band is very long. Adults have to stay vigilant. It's delightful if the parent can stay close, but allow the child to explore freely.

Climbing

This is the age of exploration. Like the mountain climber, the child will scale every large object "because it's there." It's advisable to have some safe things for children to climb on like a low climber designed for young toddlers or a large, soft chair or couch. Supervise, and place soft padding material underneath.

Climbing Stairs

Crawling up stairs now is a full-fledged compulsion. At home, there is nothing that a baby enjoys more than crawling up and down a flight of stairs with an adult right behind. Stairways need to be blocked off with gates for safety when an adult is not there to supervise this compulsion. A small nursery set of stable wooden steps will find much interest from older infants and young toddlers.

Pushing and Pulling

Once a child can walk, push toys and pull toys are very popular. They give children something to do with their new skill, and to a certain degree motivate the child to practice the skill. (Do be assured that the child would be driven to walk without these toys.) These toys are also good because they usually make a fine noise, and let the child practice the cause and effect phenomenon.

Practice Moving in Different Ways

Now children have quite a repertoire of ways to move across a space. They will be kept happily occupied if a teacher focuses on giving them many interesting opportunities to use all their new skills. You can count on this little person to crawl into every space where he can fit (and try to get into some places where he will not fit).

Mini Obstacle Course

See if you can arrange mini obstacle courses for babies to crawl through, climb over, etc. Such things as fabric tunnels, sheets draped over chairs and small tables, grocery boxes, small sturdy stairs and toddler slides, pillows, round bolsters, etc. can combine to make fun places to move over, through and under.

Avoid "Baby Traps"

As mentioned in the last chapter, there are many manufactured devices designed to confine babies and keep them out of harm's way. Examples are wind-up swings, bounce seats, walkers, rings to prop children up in a sitting position. All of these devices inhibit a child's use of his muscles and thus severely limit a child's opportunities to learn the new physical motor skills. While some of these devices claim that they promote the child's learning of motor skills, the opposite is true. In order for a child to learn to sit up, stand, walk, and jump, he needs to find his own balance, and use his muscles to develop strength and coordination. While some of these devices may have limited use in a home setting where a parent cannot be constantly close at hand while occupied with other things, such as making dinner, they have no place in child care situations where someone is supposed to be supervising children at all times and providing interesting things for the children to do.

FINE MOTOR DEVELOPMENT

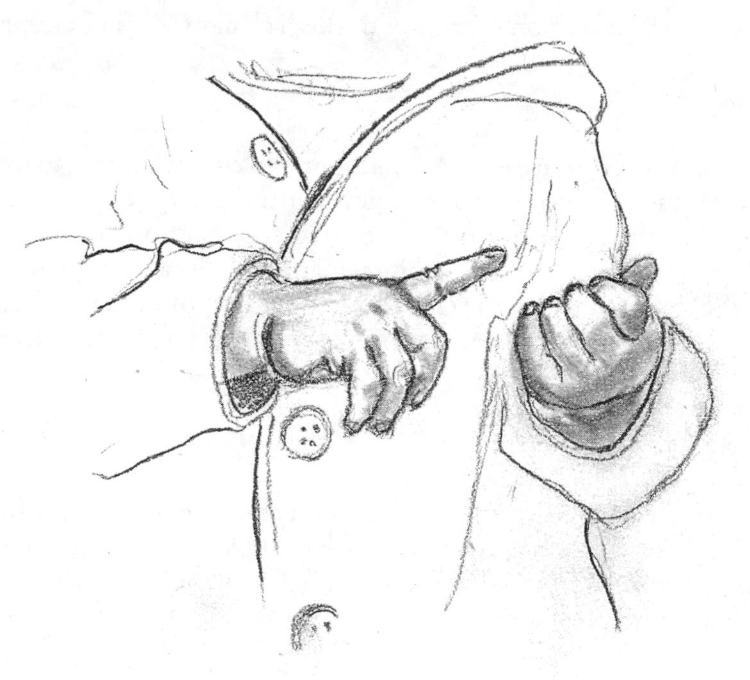

Visually Directed Reaching

At around six months the baby is gaining skill in spotting something within reach, opening his hand before it makes contact with the object, and closing his fingers at the right time to grasp the object. A younger child could grasp things, but the timing of opening and closing fingers was not well-refined. Often the child would just bump or bat at objects and not actually get hold of them. Now the child can plan the action and carry it out. It is a major step in gaining control of the world.

Picking Up Objects

First they use a raking motion to pick up small objects. All their fingers move together. This is, at best, an inefficient way to pick things up. Then, they get the pincer muscles of thumb and forefinger to cooperate and pick up small objects. At around ten months the children become able to pick up very small objects like the tiniest piece of lint or a small bug. Remove from the environment tiny objects like staples, thumb tacks, pebbles, insects and small clumps of dirt that babies this age love to pick up and put in their mouths.

Small finger foods such as dry cereal, cooked peas and cooked apple chunks to pick up and eat are great for children this age. Of course, these should be placed on the tray of the high chair or other clean surface.

Pointing

As they approach the age of one, babies seem to enjoy pointing to objects with their index finger, using their new control of this individual digit. This universal gesture has a decided connection to language development. When the child points, helpful adults are happy to name what the child points at. The child figures out his power in the situation and points some more to get a response from the adult, and eventually repeats the sound he hears.

Poking Fingers in Holes

An extension of pointing, the one-year-old also loves to stick his fingers in holes. Look for toys and books that have holes in them designed for this purpose. Lacy fabrics, "found" materials with holes, and household objects with holes will serve the purpose as well.

LANGUAGE DEVELOPMENT

This non-verbal child is by no means silent! This is the wonderful stage of babbling or jargon talk. The child will carry on, creating the most marvelous string of sounds, getting ready to utter his first words in months to come. In this critical stage of language development the child is practicing the sounds and intonations of his native language. Occasionally you will hear an almost recognizable word slip in. It is as though the child is pretending to talk. He probably has sensory pleasure having sounds come out of his mouth.

When the child babbles and coos, answer him in like fashion. Try to imitate his sounds. This social child will undoubtedly enjoy the interchange, and you are modeling the give and take of conversation. The child is learning that language is a social tool as well as a means of getting what you want.

Talk a lot! Surround the child with meaningful language about what he is seeing in front of him. Describe everything that you are doing with him. Children learn to understand language much earlier than they learn to speak. You are providing a very important model for sounds and intonations while you are providing names for objects and actions. Children show that they understand their first words in this stage. They often don't produce words until much later.

"Where's..."

Try asking, "Where's Mommy?" while you are holding the child and his mother is close by, and there are several other people in the room to choose from. If he turns to his mother and smiles, you have an indication that he knows what that particular combination of sounds means. Try this with other familiar people.

Action Commands

Try giving children simple commands such as "Wave bye-bye," "Give me a hug," "Sit down," and "Come here." Of course, you will express pleasure when the child complies.

Speak "Parentese." When parents instinctively slow down, simplify their speech and raise the pitch of their voice a little, babies "tune-in" better to this type of speech.

Among the first words a child typically learns are "mommy," "daddy," "bye-bye," and "baby," as well as social greetings, such as "Hi!"

Early Literacy

Start now to build in an addiction to books. Early exposure to appropriate books helps to create eager and competent readers in later years. You are building in a positive attitude about reading. The child learns that books are fun, full of interesting surprises, and a good way to build social contacts with favorite adults. When the child looks at bright, easy-to-recognize pictures of things he has seen, he learns that pictures are symbols that represent real things. Books with pictures of familiar objects can reinforce a child's vocabulary of words he understands and later names.

What Makes a Good Book for this Age?

Although you will want to keep certain books special and only show them to children when they are on your lap and you can insure gentle handling, children should have books they can carry around and handle themselves. Sturdy toddler board books, or some of the homemade books described below, give children pictures to look at and later name. The beauty of homemade books is that you can tailor them to the vocabulary and interests of particular children.

Zip Closure Bag Books

Sew together four or five sandwich size plastic bags with zip closures along the bottom edge. A simple whip stitch works well. Cut pieces of light cardboard to just fit inside the bags. This will stiffen the pages and make them easier to turn while providing a background for pictures you insert. Cut pictures from magazines and slip them on both sides of the cardboard in the bags.

Photo Album Book

Spiral-bound photo albums with magnetic plastic film over cardboard pages make excellent homemade books for toddlers. Photos or magazine pictures placed in the pages can be changed from time to time to keep interest high. The stiff, sturdy pages are easy for toddlers to turn.

COGNITIVE DEVELOPMENT

Cognitive development means learning how the world works, what fits where, how to make things happen, that things have shapes and move in predictable ways. You can almost see the wheels turning in the child's mind as the young child ventures out to investigate everything in his path.

Exploring Objects

Once the child gets good at visually directed reaching and can crawl around the room, the world is his to explore! The excitement is quite visible.

A child this age very much likes to examine small objects and toys, especially those that make a noise. He will typically hold an object with both hands and put it in his mouth. He will pass the object from one hand to the other and turn it around to see all sides. It will go into the mouth several times in the process. The child will also probably bang the object against a surface to see what kind of noise it makes. It is as if this junior scientist is making an investigation to find out all the possible properties and uses for this strange thing. He is learning how objects move, and about shapes and forms and textures.

All kinds of objects are interesting to children this age, not just toys. Small boxes, jar lids, keys, you name it. In addition to the usual array of toys, bring in interesting household objects such as a rubber glove, a wooden spoon, a pineapple. Offer experiences with many different textures, shapes and weights of objects.

Object Permanence

One of the interesting developments toward the end of this stage is "object permanence." Up until about eight months, if something left the baby's field of vision, it ceased to exist in the mind of the child. "Out of sight, out of mind." You can see this if you catch a younger child's attention with an attractive new object, just out of reach. Cover the object up, and the child will not try to look for it or remove the barrier between himself and the toy. When a child develops object permanence, he will try to pull away the covering to get at the object again.

Developing object permanence is a very significant mental development. It means that the child can retain a mental image of an object that is not within sight. It is the very beginning of abstract thought, which is the basis for the development of imagination, fantasy play, and using symbols to represent objects, as in reading.

Like so many developments in the first years, object permanence is not something you must teach babies. It happens by itself...probably when the child's neurological development is at the right point. But once you recognize this as an emerging skill you can have lots of fun with it. There are many games playing with object permanence that children will enjoy for quite a time to come.

Hide and Seek

Play simple versions of hide and seek. Hide yourself behind a chair with a good part of you sticking out in view. Say, "Where am I?"... "Here I am!" Soon the child will be able to come after you.

Peek-A-Boo Variations

- *Simply put your hands in front of your face, and remove them, saying "peek-a-boo!"*
- *Pop up and down from behind a divider or piece of furniture.*
- *Put a scarf over your head and pull it off, saying "peek-a-boo."*
- *Put the scarf over the child's head and pull it off, saying "peek-a-boo."*
- *Have a stuffed animal or puppet play peek-a-boo.*
- *Put stuffed animals inside boxes with lids for children to open and discover. Put the lid back on and say "Bye-bye." Uncover again. Repeat.*
- *Turning the pages of a book back and forth has a peek-a-boo appeal. Pictures disappear and reappear.*

Cause and Effect

The child is fascinated by cause and effect relationships. Action A causes response B. Mobile infants especially like toys that do something when they act on them. If the toy makes a noise, if it has a moving part, if something happens, the toy holds his attention longer. Of course, this is the time children learn the fun of dropping things from a highchair tray. The child is learning he can make something happen in the world and repeat the effect, gaining a sense of personal power. Shaker toys (rattles) are great for this age. Safe squeeze toys that squeak are fun, too.

A Shake-shake Collection

Make a collection of toys that make a noise when they are shaken. There are, of course, many ways to make these from cans with plastic lids and boxes. A coffee can with a clothespin inside will sound different from a spice can with grains of rice inside. The child will enjoy exploring the differences.

Make sure tops remain securely fastened so that the child does not swallow what's inside. Children will enjoy this type of collection from now on through the toddler years.

Using Symbols

In late infancy, children can recognize pictures in a book. They might look at the illustration or photo of a dog, and then turn and point to a real dog in the room. They have figured out that this shape on the paper represents something else that is real. A photo album containing pictures of people the child knows is good to have around for the child to enjoy.

A toy is another kind of symbol. You often see a child this age hold a toy telephone up to his ear. He might pretend to drink from a doll's baby bottle or use a toy camera to snap pictures.

MUSIC

When the baby babbles away, is he talking or singing? Probably both. The child is really learning to use his voice in many different ways.

La, la, la

Try singing two or three notes over and over just saying "la" and see if the child comes close to imitating your chant.

If you sing a lot, the child will learn that singing is one thing people do with their voices, and it is more likely to become part of his early repertoire of things to do with his voice.

Sing Talking

Sing about what you and the baby are doing. Pick any familiar melody and make up your own words. Don't worry about rhyme. You will find places to repeat words. For instance, to the tune of "Here We Go 'Round the Mulberry Bush": "We're putting a new diaper on, diaper on, diaper on. We're putting a new diaper on, so now you will be dry."

Dancing

Put on some lively music and children cannot stand still! In their wide stance they will rock from side to side. Or some will bend their knees and bounce up and down. Balance, coordination, and fun!

HOW THEY PLAY

Solitary play is the main mode for our explorers. Their main focus is on objects as well as using their new gross-motor skills by themselves. They engage in "object play" performing endless experiments to gain physical knowledge about the objects, whatever they are. Their physical play consists of trying new movements over and over again – crawling over a small set of steps, rolling, picking things up and dropping them, pulling up to standing and squatting down over and over again.

Even though they are independently occupied in these pursuits, they will watch other children with interest, and toward the end of this stage may imitate what another child is doing. Stay close to facilitate successful play near other children.

The Play Environment

Making the Environment Safe

This age child will fully examine every object, which until now he has only been able to see, and not touch. He will put everything possible in his mouth and lick and suck on everything else. This is a good time to do a thorough check of your environment to make sure there are no dangerous things for a child to handle. Dangling cords from such things as irons at home, and radios and clocks on shelves are hazards sometimes overlooked by adults. Make sure safety caps are inserted in all electrical outlets within reach of a crawling baby. (Please see the "Safety" Appendix at the end of book.)

This is the time when many babies come into direct conflict with adults. It is generally advised that parents clear the decks as much as possible of breakable or otherwise forbidden objects. If a child hears too many "no's" at this time he may become even more rebellious in the coming toddler age, or worse, may become compliant but lose some of the natural curiosity of young children. A child's curiosity and initiative in exploring has a relationship to the development of intelligence. Most child care environments are (or should be) set up so that everything in the child's environment is available and safe for examination. In this "yes" environment, children can investigate to their heart's content. The teacher's job is to provide interesting new things to explore from time to time, and to maintain a safe environment.

Inside Play Area

Access is the first concern. Make sure these exploring infants have plenty of time on the floor, free to use muscles and practice their new skills. Have a safe, easy to supervise area divided off from the rest of your environment. If you have younger infants in the group as well, create a divided off space for them so these eager explorers won't overwhelm them.

Since new motor skills are dominating, create interesting surfaces, angles and textures for them to explore as they crawl about, as well as nooks and crannies to crawl in and out of. A safe thing to climb on is a necessity. Interesting cause and effect toys as well as safe everyday objects to examine are also important. Create enough space and comfort so that an adult can settle down in the play area to supervise and interact with the babies whenever possible.

Going Outside

The outdoor environment can offer many rich sensory experiences and opportunities for active play, and you don't need a very large area. Grass and shade are needed. This would be a good place to offer water play using a dishpan.

SUMMARY

Responsive physical care. These babies still need, most of all, a warm, loving, responsive adult – a personal relationship with a cherished caregiver.

In order to venture out into the wide world of discovery, they need a feeling of comfort and security with their caregiver. The caregiver must express pride in the child's new accomplishments and encourage an eager, "greet the world" attitude.

Opportunities to move. Children this age need the opportunity to practice new physical skills. They need space in a safe, open environment to do this. In this time of major physical development, the child must have a chance to use his muscles. Babies who are awake should not be kept in cribs, but allowed to wiggle, roll and sit up and crawl around on a clean floor.

They should be offered many interesting objects to examine and explore to feed their developing curiosity. Make the infant's world an interesting place.

CHAPTER 3

The Toddler

THERE IS PROBABLY no "cuter," and no more difficult stage to be with all day long than the toddler between one and two years of age. The toddler is totally lovable and engaging, curious and "into everything," egocentric, demanding, extreme in moods, and high in energy. It may be very tiring and even exasperating at times dealing with toddlers day in and day out. But it's such a fascinating age! So much progress is made in such a short time. Toddlers are in the act of discovering the world. Now that they can walk, the world is theirs to possess!

SOCIAL EMOTIONAL DEVELOPMENT

Issues of Emotional Development and Self-esteem

Toddlers are not as easy to cuddle as they were a few months ago. They will be hugged and "loved" on their own terms only. Too busy.

Independence

With their new ability to walk, comes the taste of "freedom." Off they go! This is the age of the drive for independence. "Me do it byself!!!" The child is in a constant drive to establish herself as a separate individual. Therefore she pushes away from her mother and caregiver, and resists suggestions. "No" is one of her first words. Loud protests are common. The confusing thing is that this same contrary, independent little person is often suddenly clinging, climbing on laps, asking for help, and generally very cuddly and cozy. Back and forth. The child frequently needs to go back to "home base," the trusted adult, to re-establish a feeling of security before again venturing out.

In dealing with a toddler's independence and contrariness it's best to avoid a showdown. Instead of telling a child to do something, or asking if she would like to (a sure way to get a "no" response), offer two "yes" choices. "Would you like apples or oranges for snack?"

Develop a consistent daily routine, doing things in the same order every day. If you go outside every day after snack, children will often go over to get their coats on without prompting. Within your consistent order of events, leave the bulk of your day fairly unstructured, allowing children to play where they choose. If you bring out a special toy or activity, it will attract children without a lot of directives from you.

Separation Difficulties

Being separated from parents or special adults is a big issue for toddlers, which seems ironic because of the drive for autonomy described above. They only feel safe to "venture out" if that adult is nearby. They feel very vulnerable when they are separated. It also has to do with power. This toddler may have tried everything she could to make the parent stay – sad looks, hanging on, crying, even kicking and screaming in protest, and the parent still leaves. So there is outrage as well as fear.

It can be a difficult time to begin using child care outside the home. Most people report success when the transition is gradual. Start by having the parent and the child visit the program together, playing and enjoying the environment and the other children. The parent can speak positively about this at home, remembering the fun they had. On a subsequent visit, have the parent leave the room briefly, first just for a few minutes and then return. He or she should tell the child, "I'm leaving now, but I'll be back in a few minutes." Return promptly, and say, "See, I came back."

The parent should never sneak away while the child isn't looking. This betrays the child's trust and will make her even more anxious in the future. Instead, create a comforting ritual for saying good-bye; for instance, one twirl around, a hug, two kisses, and then wave good-bye again through the window. This type of ritual gives the child a small sense of control – she knows what is going to happen.

When the parent leaves and the distressed toddler cries, don't brush away her sadness and try to distract her immediately. Instead, comfort her and model empathy. Acknowledge what she is feeling so she knows she has been heard and respected. "It's hard to say good-bye in the morning. I am here to take good care of you until your daddy comes back after lunch." Other children may come over and watch with concern on their faces. You can say, "Tasha is crying because she is sad that her daddy left. What can you think of that might make her feel better?" Other children might offer a hug or bring a blanket. Of course, have interesting things to do set up, so that the child can enter into play on her own terms.

Good-bye Books

Have a special set of books for parents and children to choose from. At parting time in the morning, the parent allows the child to choose a book that she will read to the child when she returns. This book is put in the child's cubby. During the day it is a constant, physical reminder that the parent will return, because she said she would read this book. As part of the reunion at pick-up time, the parent and child sit down and enjoy the book together – a great way to "reconnect."

Souvenir Photos

Toddlers can find it very comforting to have photos of parents to carry around with them during the day. A small photo album or photos laminated or encased in clear contact paper work well.

Transitional Objects

Many toddlers are comforted by a special blanket or stuffed animal whose presence gives them the courage to go out and meet the world. Other children learn to respect these. "That is Jackson's special bear. He doesn't have to share that." Often, once children feel comfortable in a new situation, they can leave their security object in their cubby for most of the day, bringing it out only at nap time. This is one of the first "symbols" a child invents and uses. It is a physical reminder of home.

Comfort in Sameness

Toddlers don't like change. They like to feel comfortable in knowing what is going to happen next. You can eliminate a lot of problems by having a good, solid basic routine. Your routine can be augmented by "rituals." Rituals are little things that are done day in and day out in exactly the same way. They can be a way of saying, "All's right with the world." Your puppet comes out first thing every morning and says good morning to everyone. You put on the same recording of march music every day at clean-up time. You say the same poem each day before lunch. You tuck in each child individually and sing the same lullaby at nap time. When children get comfortable with rituals, it will be easier to teach them such things as washing hands after being diapered and before eating and hanging up their coat when they come inside.

Relationships With Other Children

Exploration

Often young toddlers will treat other children like objects or toys put there for their examination, and poke eyes, pull hair, etc. These gestures may not be meant to hurt the other child; the toddler doesn't really realize that other people can feel "hurt." Rather, they do these things to explore what the other "child-object" is good for, e.g., interesting noises, etc.

Empathy

This is the time to start teaching children about kindness and empathy. Actually, there can be surprising touches of empathy in toddlers. If a child in the room hurts herself or cries, another toddler may come over and try to comfort her. She may offer a toy or her blanket. This is the way a toddler would also try to comfort her tired daddy – with something the toddler would be comforted with herself. This behavior is not consistent. The same toddler may comfort a child once, and ignore distress another time. Children learn about empathy by seeing it modeled by adults. If you and other important adults in the child's life show concern and kindness when a child is hurt, children will learn from you.

Toddler Friendships

Toddlers do like playing near and with other children and even develop special friendships. When they see their special friend in the neighborhood or at child care, they squeal with delight and run toward each other. There may even be hugs and kisses. (See the next chapter for a discussion of early friendships.)

Typical Behavior Issues

Egocentrism

Toddlers are egocentric in their relationship to other people. Don't think of this in the negative way we use this word with adults. In a very young child, it simply means that the child has not had experience in the world of people. In the mind of the toddler, the whole world exists only for her pleasure and service. Here's a scenario: Tammy sees another child playing with an attractive toy. It looks like fun. She wants it. So she grabs the toy away from the other child. Then she is genuinely surprised that there is a protest at the other end of the toy! She thinks because she wants the toy, everybody must want her to have the toy. She does not yet understand that other people can have a different opinion of how things should be. The ongoing task of the parent or caregiver is to point out how the other child feels.

Toddler Aggression

Toddlers are very demanding and they can become frustrated very quickly. They don't have words to get what they want or even express their frustration, so they take action physically. When a child this age acts with aggression, it does not mean that he is destined to carry a switch-blade. It is very likely a "stage" in the truest sense of the word.

Prevention is the best tactic, of course, but not always possible. If you see frustration building, step in quickly. Try to teach the child to use words, although with some toddlers this is a long way off. Anticipate. Childproof the environment. Tell children how you want them to behave beforehand.

When a toddler hurts another child it is important to react with clarity. Come over quickly. Comfort the victim, and state very strongly to the aggressor child that it is not okay to hurt people. If the child has scratched another child, for instance, bring her face to face with the victim. Show the marks. Say, "Look! You hurt Joey! Look at his eyes...he's crying because it hurts. It's not okay to hurt people. I don't want you to scratch anymore." Don't worry if you think the child will not understand all your words. Your facial expression and tone of voice will communicate your meaning. Be serious and stern without yelling. When you yell, the child becomes frightened and all other messages are lost. It may help to have the aggressor go with you to get a cloth to wash off the scratch. She should see you comforting the victim. This advice goes for all kinds of hurting – hitting, biting, scratching, hair pulling, pushing, poking, etc.

Do not ignore hurting behaviors in hopes that they will go away by themselves. If you ignore aggression, younger children will think you approve of it. Even other children in the room will think you approve if you do not react to the aggressor.

Do not react to a child's aggression against other children by physically punishing the child. Remember, a toddler's main method of learning social behaviors is imitating the important adults in her life. If you slap or spank a child, she will become more aggressive. If you show the child how to react with kindness, she will learn kindness. Unfortunately, this does not happen overnight. You must remain vigilant and consistent.

Biting

Biting is, unfortunately, not an uncommon behavior of toddlers. It is the most distressing form of aggression. Often biting occurs only when the toddler finds herself in a group of other children, but not at home.

There are a number of things that might lead to biting. You start from the probable reason and then try to give the child a more acceptable way of getting her needs met.

• Teething. Toddlers are cutting teeth and it hurts. Chewing on something makes it feel better. Since there are so many other things to chew on, teething is probably not the reason toddlers bite other children. Have things that are okay to bite. Keep a bowl of carrot sticks around. Tell a child, "If you need to bite something, tell me, and I'll get you a carrot stick." You could keep small sponges in zip closure plastic bags in the refrigerator for this purpose. Or, put clean wash cloths, which were wet and wrung out, in the freezer. Above all, stay alert and perceptive of children's teething distress.

• Sensory exploration. This is a very "oral" stage of development. They chew on everything, not just their fellow man. Sometimes children bite a child who is new to the group as a way to find out more about them. Give children plenty of opportunities to release tension through tactile experiences. Water play is especially soothing. Play dough also allows children to squeeze out tensions. As for the new child, encourage the other children to come over to her and see her and touch her while you are right there (not all at once, of course). It may help.

• Cause and effect. It's almost like their interest in something like a jack-in-the-box toy. Young toddlers are constantly studying cause and effect and are amazed to find out that they have the power to make something happen. With biting, an action produces a predictable response – and what a response! There are many ways you can allow children to cause legitimate effects on their environment. Of course, if you perceive the effect they're after is to get your attention, that's another matter. The obvious, and overly simple, answer is to give them more attention. Look at children. Use their names. Smile. Pick them up and waltz with them for no apparent reason before they bite.

• Mimicking. This may be why after a long period of no biting, you suddenly have a rash of biting in the program. Children learn behaviors from other children. The only thing you can do is give a strong message that this behavior is not approved, and give them lots of positive behaviors to imitate instead.

• Frustration. This is the main reason toddlers bite. Self-assertion. Instant power! It's a way to express frustration when they don't yet have the language skills to do so. Biting, a child learns, is the quickest and most efficient way to register a protest. First, take a good critical look at your program and try to cut down on frustration to toddlers. Avoid crowding children. Keep them happily occupied with interesting activities and they are less likely to bite. Work diligently and daily on building children's verbal communication skills – both in giving messages and receiving messages. "Johnny, say 'Stop – don't hit me!'" "Tell her with words instead of screams, Jenny. Say, 'I'm using this now.'" "Jason, do you hear Jenny? She said 'Mine.' That means she's using that now. You can have it when she's through. Here's another puzzle you can use."

If you see frustration building in a child – grabbing toys or fighting with other children, screaming, whining, tantrums, etc. – redirect the child. Intervene, and get her involved in something else.

Involve the biter in comforting the victim. Model an empathetic response to the victim. Show concern for the hurt. Let the biter see you hug the victim and say you are sorry that happened to her. Say out loud, "Let's see what we can do to make the hurt go away." You can invite the biter to get a cold cloth to put on the bruised area, or find the victim's special security toy to bring to her to make her feel better. Just be careful that the biter isn't so enjoying the extra attention that she is getting as "the comforting one" that she bites again in order to play the role. If you sense that is what is going on, it is clear that the biter needs more positive attention from you in non-aggressive situations.

Ease the re-entry. Involve the biter in something totally different from what she was doing before – something soothing like play dough. You need to get this child back into a positive mode as quickly as possible. When you have a few minutes, settle down for some one-on-one play with the child, without stating or implying it is because she bit someone earlier. You need to re-establish a positive relationship with this child.

The real key to preventing biting in your program is to keep children busy and happy, touch and hug them a lot, cut down on toddler frustration, and give them a lot of individual attention. There is more biting when the group size is larger, so divide the children into smaller groups. Do what you can to develop empathy in toddlers by describing feelings of other children...all sorts of feelings. Notice positive behaviors: "You wanted that doll, Jenny, but you waited for Latoya to finish. Good job!" "Good talking, Joe! You used words to tell her what you want."

Difficulty Sharing

Don't expect toddlers to share naturally. We must again go back to their egocentricity. They simply cannot put themselves in another person's shoes. Yet there is much adults can do to guide the child in this direction.

Consciously model sharing behavior yourself, and talk about it. "I brought some graham crackers and I'm going to share them with all of you." "Come over here, Sheila. I will share my play dough with you." They have to know what the word "share" means before they can learn to do it. Later you can ask, "Sheldon, will you share your play dough with me? Thank you! That makes me happy." Next, judging the mood and likelihood for success, you can ask a child, "Jennifer, will you share your play dough with Seth? He doesn't have any." Express appreciation if there is compliance. "I bet Seth is happy." By all means, if you notice rare spontaneous sharing, draw subtle attention to it. "Tamara felt happy when you let her have some of the blocks."

Give children successful experiences sharing by setting up situations where sharing is easy. For instance, put a bowl of crayons between two children who are coloring and say, "You two can share these crayons." Other materials that have many pieces are also good for this, such as fit-together toys, extra large pegs or beads to string.

Tantrums

Because children at this age have few words to express frustrations, and very little actual power, they often resort to tantrums, or emotional "melt-downs." Toddlers are people of extremes. A polite protest is often not within their range of social responses. Even the slightest annoyance may lead to kicking and screaming. Treat the tantrum with patience – don't match it – and let the child see that it will not help her get her way.

When a child begins a tantrum because she cannot have what another child is playing with, for instance, you might bring a pillow or two to where the child is and say matter-of-factly, "I see you are very upset. When you are finished and calm down, we can talk about what to do. We're all going over there to play now because this noise hurts our ears."

Short Attention Span

One difficulty in dealing with a group of toddlers is their extremely short attention span. They are easily distracted. "A lick and a promise" is all they give most activities. The world is just too exciting to spend much time doing just one thing.

Their very "distractability" can work to your advantage when the child is being difficult. If the child is demanding a certain object, for instance, her attention can be quite easily diverted to another interesting object.

There are a few techniques that help keep the attention of toddlers for a few minutes longer.

• The "flop down and do" technique. Instead of calling toddlers over and trying to get them all to sit down and pay attention at the same time, simply flop down on the floor and start doing whatever it was you wanted to present to them. At first, two or three children will see you and come over. Then more children will want to get in on the action. They stay longer when it was their choice to come over in the first place.

• Entice children over with a novelty. Bring out something different that they haven't seen that day. A music box they haven't heard will stop everyone dead in their tracks! See the "Surprise Bag" activity described in the next chapter. This works like magic with toddlers.

• Do simple art projects with only a few children at a time. Set up the activity for one child, and have paper and crayons available for a few "watchers" while they wait their turn. (Have other activities the "watchers" could be doing elsewhere in the room if they wish. They should be there by free choice.) Whether it is finger painting, painting with a brush, or scribbling, the artist won't take long, and the watchers are gaining experience.

GROSS MOTOR DEVELOPMENT

Toddlers "toddle." They stand and walk with feet wide apart and arms out from the side or bent upward for balance. They often walk while holding onto objects in each hand, as though for security. It doesn't take long for toddlers to gain skill at getting up and down from the floor quickly, and squatting. They enjoy bending over and looking at the world from between their legs.

Once the child learns to walk, the next step is to run! There is the insatiable drive to explore every space and climb everything climbable. There are plenty of stumbles and falls as the child develops competency on her feet. Gross-motor activity, using large muscles of arms, legs and trunk, is clearly the most dominant drive of toddlers. Their energy is incredible. They spend a lot of time just wandering from one object to another in the room.

They hate being confined – in a playpen, car seat, crib or highchair. This is the age when they will learn to climb out of almost anything and free themselves from constraints like an escape artist, and as a result sometimes experience serious falls. In a child care setting, for safety as well as accommodating the child's growing autonomy, this is a good time to start seating children on small chairs at low tables for meals, instead of in highchairs, and sleeping on cots or mats rather than in cribs.

Climbing

It is highly advisable to have a stable, toddler-sized climbing apparatus in the room. That will make it easier to redirect them from climbing on chairs, tables, and shelves.

Playing with Balls

Balls of all kinds are great for toddlers. Make a collection and see how many different types you can find. Inflatable beach balls are especially good because they are big and the child feels powerful being able to pick up something so large. Although toddlers are not good at kicking a ball because it is too difficult to balance on one foot while swinging the other, they sort of run into balls or shove them to make them move.

Throwing

Throwing is a new discovery of physics for a toddler. They find out that if they get their arm moving and open their fingers at a certain time, the object they are holding will sail through the air. They have to test this on all sorts of things.

Toddler Basketball

Toddlers enjoy throwing things but have minimal skill hitting a target. The teacher can hold out a large plastic laundry basket and catch balls thrown by toddlers in her general direction from three or four feet away.

Soft Ball

Toddlers' compulsion for throwing can be safely met indoors or outdoors with this simple to make ball. Simply stuff polyester fiberfill stuffing into a double layer of nylon stocking and knot at both ends. Support hose last a little longer. These will not hurt people or objects when thrown. They can also be thrown into the washer and dryer. While one or two of these are fun, lots and lots of them are wonderful.

Stacking

Stacking things up and knocking them down again is lots of fun. Empty food boxes from the pantry will do. Cardboard blocks are popular in toddler programs because they are light and manageable by toddlers.

Cardboard Box Blocks

Let toddlers help you wad up newspaper and stuff it into large cardboard boxes. Then tape the boxes shut. Now you have very large, light-weight blocks that toddlers love to lift and stack. They feel very powerful being able to lift something big.

Imitation Games

Follow-the-leader games, with the teacher leading, are very successful with toddlers. They will enjoy imitating almost any movement you can think up.

Toys That Move

Pull toys and push toys that make a noise appeal to toddlers, and they can use them on the move. Often you'll see a little dramatic play as they use push toys, pretending they are lawn mowers or vacuum cleaners. Attach a string to a box and you have a very simple pull toy that the toddler can drag around, and use to give rides to stuffed animals and dolls.

Riding Toys

Toddlers love to sit on small wheeled toys and propel themselves by pushing their feet on the ground. Have several because toddlers love doing the same thing as their friends, and riding toys are one of the things they fight over most frequently.

FINE MOTOR DEVELOPMENT

Toddlers enjoy handling objects. As well as putting things in their mouths, they will examine an object from all sides, then try to figure out all the different things one can do with it. Rotating their wrists to manipulate objects is a new, not-well-developed skill. This is an important skill in learning to put puzzles together. Wooden inlay puzzles with single shapes are good starters. Some come with large knobs, making it easy for toddlers to grasp pieces.

Sticking Things in Holes

Toddlers find holes irresistible. The traditional "shape boxes" are challenging and difficult for them. First they have to perceive the shape of the hole and how it relates to the three dimensional shape of the solid piece. When that is accomplished (often not until late in the toddler year) the child must hold the piece and rotate her wrist just right, as with puzzles, to make the piece fit. Often she will just try to jam it through the hole.

Simple Shape Box

To make a less frustrating "beginner's shape box" simply cut a round hole in a coffee can lid. The child will enjoy sticking all manner of small objects through the hole.

Slot Boxes

Boxes with slots in them are fun. Toddlers will enjoy putting pieces of junk mail through a slot in a cardboard "mailbox." Or, cut a slot in the top of a used diaper wipes box and let the child stick baby food jar lids through it, open it and dump it out again.

Fit-together Toys

Toys with projections and indentations, such as the toddler versions of molded plastic bricks, allow the child to line things up, exert pressure, and create new shapes. These will attract momentary interest from young toddlers but they won't build something. They'll just explore the spaces. Make sure the pieces are at least the size of a fist so toddlers cannot choke on them. Don't use plastic brick type construction toys that are designed for older children. Toddlers will be much more interested in a collection of "found" objects that they can fit things through, and open and close.

Stacking and Nesting Toys

Toddlers are interested in combining things in different ways. The child makes exciting discoveries about shape and volume. Start by giving the child plastic bowls of the same size. These are the easiest nesting toys, because they will fit together in any order. They will interest young toddlers because they look so different when they are nested together from when they are separate, and spread out in front of the toddlers. Later offer bowls or cubes of graduated sizes.

Screwing on Jar Lids

Look for a plastic jar with a lid a child can grasp, but one too large to choke on. The child can practice her new skill of rotating her wrist.

Dumping

Emptying and filling things becomes a passion with toddlers, and yes, they do more emptying than filling! Light plastic shovels and sand pails, or margarine tubs and scoops from coffee cans will get much eager use in a sandbox. Dumping can be refined to pouring. Playing with water is a compulsion with toddlers. A dishpan of water with a few plastic cups, a small pitcher, small plastic bottles and other containers will get the concentrated attention of toddlers.

Art Activities

Many "art" projects give toddlers a chance to practice their fine-motor skills: play dough (the all-time toddler favorite), finger painting, brush painting, pasting, scribbling, etc. They can grasp a fat crayon using a clumsy full fist hold and enjoy scribbling.

LANGUAGE DEVELOPMENT

It's getting interesting now. The "jargon" or random babbling and stringing together of nonsense syllables of earlier stages continues. This babbling is really an "alphabet soup" as children practice all the sounds, intonations and rhythms of their native language. Although toddlers vary greatly in their production of speech, most are coming out with their first words at this time. There will be an exciting span of time when a child seems to be saying new words almost every day. Also, you will be aware that children are understanding more and more of what you say to them.

Children usually start by naming familiar objects and saying common social phrases: "Mama," "Doggie," "Spoon," "Bye-bye!" "Hi!" "Night-night," "Mine!" "Thank you!" Soon two-word phrases emerge: "My ball," "Mo juice!" Of course, pronunciation is not accurate at this stage. Don't worry about it or make any attempt to correct pronunciation. Do speak clearly yourself, though. "Baby talk" was fine for its social aspects in the first year of the child's life. Now it's best to model the correct pronunciation of words.

The Envelope of Language

The best way to enhance language development is to provide a good "envelope of language," surrounding the child with meaningful talk.

Just having a lot of language around children is not sufficient. "Canned language" from a radio or TV doesn't count. The talk must be from a live human being, and it must be about the here and now. Two adults talking about what they did yesterday will have little meaning for the toddler. But if you talk about what the child sees going on in front of her, understanding of language will be enriched.

Talk to yourself as you go about the routines of the day. Describe what you are doing. "I'm washing my hands now to get this green paint off my fingers." "I am putting the spaghetti on your plate now." And talk about what the children are doing. "Oh, Teddy fell down." "You are rocking back and forth, back and forth in the rocking chair." "Here comes Jessie, riding on the horsie." This provides the "sensory connection" that will allow the child to associate things and actions with the sounds (words) that represent them.

Expand on the child's words. The child says, "Ball!" You say, "Oh, do you want to play with the ball? I'll get it for you." This gives the children the model for putting together longer phrases and sentences eventually. They are absorbing language rules of syntax and sentence structure. These more complex sentences won't show up in children's speech for at least another year or so, but you are at the "data input" stage.

Keep in mind the difference between "receptive language" and "productive language." Receptive language is what the child hears and understands. Productive language is words and phrases the child manages to say. There is often a wide gap between the two. A child between one and two years of age understands many more words than she is able to produce in her own speech. Parents should not worry if the child is producing very few words, as long as she demonstrates that she understands things. Ask her to get you something. "Teddy, bring me the book on the table." "Close the door." "Where's the doggie?"

Comprehension Games

Body Parts

Play the "touch your nose" game, asking the child to touch various body parts, or point to people or objects in the room. "Show me your ears." "Where's your foot?"

Pack a Bag

You or a puppet could produce a small suitcase. Tell the child to go and get one object at a time to put in the suitcase. "Get me a blanket to put in my suitcase." "Thank you! Now get me a book..."

Nursery Rhymes

The old Mother Goose rhymes and the simple melodies that go with them are just right for this age. It doesn't matter that they don't understand every single word. Who does? It's the bouncy rhythms and funny sounds that are appealing. You are reinforcing the idea that language is fun to play with. Toddlers will not be able to actually recite the rhymes, but they may join in on particular phrases occasionally.

Early Literacy

There are many things adults can do to build a child's aptitude for reading, even at this early age.

- Build the child's vocabulary. Before children can interpret "talk written down," they must have a basic facility with language. The toddler year is when children start to understand and use words. Focus on introducing a wide range of words in a meaningful context.
- Love books yourself and show it. If the child sees important adults enjoying books for their own pleasure, this is likely to be imitated.
- Give the child interesting pictures to look at. Being able to "read" pictures, and see that they represent something else that is real is an early pre-reading skill.
- Read many delightful picture books to the child. The child associates reading with pleasant social interactions with favorite adults.
- Let them find things on a page. Toddlers genuinely enjoy pointing to pictures on a page in a book. "Where's the elephant?"

Books

Toddlers love books. They are full of surprises. Actually, books are an elaborate system of peek-a-boo, which we know toddlers love. Good books for toddlers have very clear, realistic, uncomplicated illustrations or photographs. Picture books with one thing on each page are good. Children also enjoy books that have an unusual shape, or are interesting to feel with various textures inside. A nicely illustrated book of nursery rhymes and simple poetry is a good addition to your book collection at this time. The pictures will enhance the enjoyment of the sounds.

Since toddlers are very rough on books, you will want to keep some books on a high shelf and only bring them out to read to children at special times. However, toddlers should also have the experience and pleasure of handling books and turning the pages themselves. Use some of the sturdy homemade alternatives described in the previous chapter.

COGNITIVE DEVELOPMENT

The development of language has a huge impact on a child's thought processes. Words become anchors for thoughts. The more the child develops language abilities in the next few years, the more effectively she will be able to think about things. Consider any language development activities to be cognitive activities as well.

The busy toddler is still investigating the world by handling every object and figuring out what fits where, what goes with what, which things are similar and which are different, and discovering the effects of their actions.

Object Permanence

Even though they have figured out that things still exist even when they are out of sight, they still enjoy experimenting with this over and over again. See the previous chapter for variations of "peek-a-boo" that toddlers will also enjoy.

Hide and Seek

Toddlers will love all the variations of "Hide and Seek" you can think of. Hide toys in the room. Place an object under a piece of fabric and let them guess what it is. Invite the child to hide herself and let others look for her.

Music Box Hide and Seek

While children are not looking, wind up a music box, and hide it somewhere in the room where children can find it. Can they follow the sound to locate the music box?

Using Symbols

Pictures are symbols that toddlers can understand.

Picture Thing Match

Make drawings or take photographs of several familiar things in the room. Show the child the picture, and play the "What's that?" game. Let the child name the thing. Then see if the child can take the picture over to the real object in the room. Do this with photos of people too, turning it into a fun social game.

Time

Toddlers live in the here and now. They are only beginning to understand the ideas, "soon," "later," "not yet." They are beginning to develop an understanding of sequencing though, that things happen in a certain order. See if they think it's funny or correct you if you put their shoes on before their socks. This is another important reason to keep the routines in your day very stable. Do the same things in the same order, at the same time every day. It will give them a sense of security to have some predictability.

Cause and Effect

Experiments in "causality" fascinate toddlers. Action A produces response B. This is an age of exploration, not only exploring every physical space, but exploring every property of every object they come across. As these little Einsteins cover the earth, nothing is safe from their experiments and investigations. Look for toys that create some noise or other effect when the child acts on it. Of course, lots of other activities provide this as well, such as all sorts of art activities and sensory play, and musical instruments!

MUSIC

Music and language production are closely related in the early years. If you sing a lot, your children will sing a lot. They will not, except in very rare cases, be able to hold a tune. Young toddlers won't even sing a song along with you, but their voices will fade in and out of your songs. Every now and then you may notice them chanting particular words or phrases as they engage in solitary play. It is not uncommon to hear a little voice sing out, "Eee-ei-ee-ei-o."

When you sing a lot, you are modeling another way to use your voice to express yourself. A room that has singing in it is usually a happy room.

Music can help to set the tone of your classroom. While not advocating a "musak" approach with constant background music, at certain times of day playing recorded music can make things go more smoothly. Happy, peppy music in the morning can make a child care center seem less empty and more cheerful. Soft classical music can calm children down before nap time.

Music for Comfort

Rocking and singing to a child who is crying and upset, perhaps because mommy just left, will often calm the child better than any words you can produce. Whereas toddlers don't always understand the meaning of the words, music communicates.

Lullabies

There is nothing nicer than having someone sing you your own personal lullaby. (Can you remember?) At nap time when children are drifting off to sleep, a gentle touch on the head or a back rub accompanied by the singing voice of a favorite grown-up gives a child a sense of security that allows her to relax and drift off.

Shake It!

They enjoy "dancing" to recorded music, rocking from side to side in their wide toddler stance, or wiggling their behinds. Give them things like small pom poms to hold and shake while they dance for extra fun.

Rhythm Instruments

Homemade and purchased noise makers and rhythm instruments will be favorite toys of toddlers and something they can enjoy successfully with others. One hint: if possible, give everyone the same kind of instrument. The sound will be richer, and there will be less fighting. By using these, they learn a little about what kind of thing makes what kind of sound. And these are great cause-and-effect toys, with sounds that vary according to how much pressure the child exerts.

HOW THEY PLAY

Very young toddlers engage mostly in "solitary" play. Of course, there are exceptions, but most often the child is in her own little world and largely ignores other children. Of course, it's pretty hard to ignore a room full of other children! Toddlers in group care tend to be more advanced in social awareness of other children.

Imitation

Their interest in other children grows as the year goes on. They watch with interest while other children play, and may move close. Their most obvious method of showing they are interested in interacting is to imitate the other child. You will often see children side by side, using the same gestures, making the same sounds.

Swarming

This is a type of "group imitation" – everybody starts doing the same thing at one time. Children do this spontaneously, without encouragement from adults. Sometimes it's fun, such as when everybody shrieks and runs after bubbles on the playground. Other times it needs management by adults, such as when everyone starts crowding around the easel when one child is trying to paint, or what one caregiver describes as "mutiny at the lunch table," when everybody starts banging their spoons or laughing. When things get too wild, you can divert them. "I know it's fun to be silly together, but let's wait till after lunch and then all do it together. Now it is time to eat."

Motor Play

Toddlers just like to use their bodies in all sorts of ways. Jumping, rolling, even falling down just for the fun of it, are examples. Here's one fun way to let them explore:

> *Big Box Play*
>
> *Large, empty cardboard boxes provide endless entertainment. Children will climb in and out of them, turn them on their side, sit in them, and push them around the room, giving dolls a ride.*

Object Play

Toddlers spend a lot of time just investigating, arranging and experimenting with objects. Understanding the cognitive learning that is going on helps us understand the fascination. Feed this type of play by providing a wide variety of interesting toys and objects.

Dramatic Play

It is in the toddler year that the child first starts to engage in dramatic play, or "pretend play," when the child starts to use one object to represent something else. We frequently see it first with a child using a toy telephone. Children will also mimic other adult behaviors they have seen often. They will carry a purse over their arm, stir a pot with a wooden spoon, wash dishes in a tub of soapy water, and tenderly cover a doll with a small blanket.

This fantasy play is a significant mental development. Children are using their minds in different, more flexible ways. Learning to imagine – the first step in stretching the human potential.

Creative and Sensory Play

Toddlers can make their first experiments with paints, with close supervision. Even though the paint you use should be non-toxic, you still don't want children eating it or sucking on brushes. Whether it involves painting or scribbling, the child is far from trying to draw or make anything recognizable at this age. Art materials fall into the category of fine-motor and cause-and-effect toys. The toddler is amazed to see, when she moves her arm, that a mark remains behind. She then experiments with different ways to make marks.

Likewise, toddlers greatly enjoy investigating the properties of sand and water and all the wonderful effects they can achieve. Splashing, pouring, filling and dumping can go on with great concentration. Stay close by, so you can prevent throwing sand or excessive splashing of water. These also tend to be relaxing activities for toddlers.

The Play Environment

The way to provide for all the compulsive behaviors of toddlers is to give them legitimate ways to do what they have to do. That means designing your environment so they can use all their motor skills, indoors and outdoors, and have lots of objects and interesting toys to manipulate. Organize the space by function. Put a climbing structure and riding toys in one part of the space and sensory play and art in another. Dramatic play equipment should be in the same place as dishes, dolls, hats and other props. Books should be in a cozy area, separated from the more active play. Toddlers have very little sense of this order. They will carry materials all over the room. However having a special place for most things will help them find favorite toys and will help keep the place organized.

Going Outside

An outside play area with grass, shade, a space for running, and something interesting and safe to climb on, is essential. A hard surface area or trail is desirable for riding toys. A sandbox with a cover will attract much interest. Your water table or dishpans of water can come outside, reducing the concern about mess.

Please read the Appendix about safety in the environment. This toddler child is very capable of getting herself into serious trouble while exploring the environment.

SUMMARY

Accommodating the child's growing drive for autonomy must be balanced with a secure routine, and clear and reasonable limits. The daily plan should allow many opportunities for toddlers to make free choices with the security of a caring adult nearby.

Toddlers need to be able to explore a safe environment and be active, developing all their new gross-motor skills. The teacher should plan an environment that is varied and interesting in the challenges it presents.

Simple activities and materials that involve "cause and effect" relationships fascinate toddlers, and give them practice in problem solving and reasoning.

The ability to understand language is growing rapidly this year. The teacher should integrate many rich language experiences into the daily routine and activities planned.

CHAPTER 4

The Two-Year-Old

SO MUCH IS HAPPENING during this year of growth and development. The most exciting area is language development and the blossoming of speech. Another interesting development is the beginning of pretend play – playing with dolls, dishes and dress-up clothes. The child is slowly becoming more aware of others and their feelings. Successful toilet learning often happens in this year.

SOCIAL EMOTIONAL DEVELOPMENT

You've heard about the "terrible twos." Well, most teachers of two-year-olds say they're not so terrible. It's just a matter of making your expectations match the capabilities of the age.

Issues of Emotional Development and Self-esteem

Stubbornness

Like toddlers, two-year-olds are still working through the "autonomy" business, establishing their independent identity. The reason they say "No!" so much is that they want to establish their separateness from their caregivers and find out what their personal power is. They can be contrary and stubborn. But sometimes they are better behaved in a child care situation than they are at home. They enjoy other children so much that they are generally cooperative with a teacher.

Try to figure out ways to give children "power." Let them move chairs around. Let them decide where to hang their paintings and give them the tape to do it themselves. Let them help decide what to do that day. "Shall I put puzzles or play dough on that table?" Let them "win" sometimes. If a child won't come over to listen to a story, don't make a big deal out of it. Entice children into activities, rather than directing them.

Adjustment Difficulties

Adjusting to a new child care setting can still be quite difficult for this age, partly because of their stubbornness, and partly because children are very strongly attached to their mothers. As with younger children, you need to let the child develop trust in you. Do not tell him to stop crying and be a big boy. Accept his sadness. Words can help at this age. "Sam is sad. He is crying because he misses his mommy." You are very likely to get empathetic responses from other children. "How can we make Sam feel better?" Comfort and reassure the child. "Mommy is coming back this afternoon after we have our snack. I am going to take good care of you, because I like you a lot." The two-year-old loves parallel play, so try to involve him in something other children are doing. Play dough or water play are often good ice breakers.

Short Attention Span

Although the attention span of two-year-olds is certainly short, it is considerably longer than that of toddlers. Keep your success ratio high by ending your group activities before their attention ends, and entice them with activities that involve several senses. Puppets are more interesting to listen to than teachers. A story is more fun with the aid of a flannel board.

Beginnings of Conscience

Two-year-olds are still very impulsive and have poorly developed control of their behavior. You might hear a child chanting "No, no, no..." to himself while right in the middle of some misdeed, like digging in a planter. He wants to do it. He knows he shouldn't. But that "No" voice hasn't gotten inside his head yet, at least not enough to stop the deed before it happens. An imaginary friend might pop up in this year to help absorb the guilt, e.g., "Benny made me do it."

Support the child's growing morality with good supervision. Self-control is still dependent upon factors outside himself – the approval or disapproval of parents and caregivers. Praise the child when you find he has complied with a rule, resisted some temptation, and generally behaved in a way that was difficult but right, such as sharing something with a friend, or backing off instead of hitting. Keep in mind also that two-year-olds are still quite egocentric and see most situations from their own point of view. You have to keep pointing out how others are feeling, even as you recognize and respect how the child in front of you views the situation.

Security Toys

A comfort object from home such as a teddy bear or a special blanket often helps two-year-olds go out into the wider world with courage. It is a physical reminder that they are loved. Often these items are put aside quickly as the child gets busy, and are mainly useful early in the morning when the child adjusts to the new setting, at nap time, at the end of the day when the child is tired, and when the child is hurt or not feeling well.

Relationships with Other Children

Budding Friendships

Two-year-olds very much enjoy the company of other children. Their developing language skills help them get along; however, much of their interaction is still non-verbal. They are drawn to children who have similar interests, who like the same activity choices. They also are attracted to children who look like them, or with whom they feel some sort of similarity. It helps if they have known each other for awhile.

At first, they may just watch other children playing and move close. Eye contact with the other child and smiles may initiate contact. They also use the humor of the absurd to get the attention of other children, such as making funny noises or unusual facial expressions. Children often seek out a particular other child, and then the two of them like to play by themselves, away from other children.

Imitation is the main language of their friendships. They consciously do things to make themselves feel similar to each other. You often see almost identical gestures or body postures between two children. One might start a very simple action, like hitting the surface of the sand with a shovel, and the other will imitate it. They might both put on hats in the dress-up corner and then both push a toy shopping cart around the room.

Invented games emerge. One child starts doing something, such as falling off a log on the playground, laughing loudly and making eye contact with other children. Soon he is joined by others, all doing the same thing.

Developing Social Skills

Some children are better than others at developing friendships. Early patterns of interacting socially carry over to later years and impact peer relations forever. Now is the time to recognize, address, and strengthen positive behaviors or change negative ones. The building blocks are laid down early. They form the foundation for building friendships later on. If a child barges into a play situation, destroying what others built, bosses or bullies other children or acts aggressively, soon other children learn to avoid that child. This snowballs. In later years this child becomes the "loner" and is generally unhappy. Children who are good "players" usually are liked and have friends. Here are some friendship skills children need:

• Learning how to enter play. The child needs to learn how to watch the others first and figure out what their play is about, then do something that fits in. Often the child will start by playing alongside the other players, gradually blending in. Older children can learn to create a role for themselves that enhances the play scenario.

• Imitating. If a child does what the other one is doing, there is likely to be acceptance.

• Expressing what they want to do. It helps if a child can tell the others his ideas.

• Listening to others. You can help a child process what another child is trying to tell him, especially since children often don't speak very clearly at this age.

Typical Behavior Issues

Hitting, grabbing toys away from other children, screaming, tantrums, stubbornness and refusing are the behavior problems most often listed by teachers of two-year-olds. These are largely behaviors that come out of frustration. Please take a look at the discussion of toddler aggression in the previous chapter. It applies equally to two-year-olds.

The development of language skills has a tremendous influence on children's ability to handle frustration. Work hard to give children words to handle their anger and help interpret children to each other. "Shawna, do you hear Maria? She is saying 'Mine!' She is playing with that right now. Let's find another one for you." "Angelo, ask Frankie, 'Can I play with that too?'" Get in there and help negotiate. You can really make a lot of progress with children in this year by getting them to express their needs. At first you will have to supply these words on the spot, as the child is building up to physical aggression. It takes lots of repetition in real-life situations. Later, the child may be able to call up these phrases by himself. Develop a sense of when to stand back and let children settle things themselves with their own form of negotiation. They do need to try out their new skills.

Group Size

Because two-year-olds need such close supervision to control impulses and come up with words, it is important to have a low adult/child ratio in a group care situation. You need to be close enough and free enough of other distractions to hear what is going on and intervene quickly.

Even more important than staff/child ratio in reducing aggression in two-year-olds is the group size. Even with plenty of adults around, there may simply be too many bodies to compete with. Children all want to do the same thing at the same time because they are impulsive at this age. They don't plan ahead. When someone does something that looks like fun, they all want to do it. It's also harder for them to form comfortable social relationships in large groups. In a small group, children get to know each other well and can more easily sense others' moods and warm up to each other.

GROSS MOTOR DEVELOPMENT

The stiff gait of the toddler is smoothing out. The child bends knees and ankles more when walking, swinging arms at his side. In fact, the two-year-old is enjoying a wide variety of movements. Teachers can concentrate on finding activities that allow children to practice moving in many different ways. Two-year-olds can jump, hop, roll and climb well.

Carrying Things

To go along with their desire for personal power, it seems, two-year-olds love to "haul" things. They like any container with a handle to carry things around in. Baskets, suitcases, push carts, briefcases, purses, lunch pails, etc. will be eagerly used in dramatic play and might even help at clean-up time.

Climbing

It is still a good idea to have a climber in the classroom. It will be much used and greatly enjoyed by children. An outdoor climber will be eagerly explored. This does take close adult supervision. Occasionally a child will climb up too high and be afraid to climb down. Instead of immediately lifting him down, tell the child where to put his hands and feet so he can make it down himself.

Creative Movement

Two-year-olds really enjoy creative movement games, exploring all the different ways they can make their bodies move. Many of these activities also involve dramatic play, pretending to be something else.

A simple follow-the-leader game will get eager participation. Simply hop, jump, tip-toe and crawl around the room and you will find children behind you doing the same thing. Outside suggest simple things like, "Let's pretend to be birds!" and "fly" around the playground. If you are fortunate enough to have a slight incline in the yard, children will love rolling down it. Rolling provides good torso muscle exercise.

<u>*Balloon Tennis*</u>

Open out a wire coat hanger into a square, as illustrated. Stretch a cut off piece of pantyhose over it and tape it to the handle. Straighten the handle out and cover thickly with duct tape so that there are no sharp, pointed ends.

Blow up some balloons and tie them off. Then stuff the balloons into the cut off legs of pantyhose. (This is a safety precaution. If the balloon breaks children will not have access to the balloon rubber that they could choke on.) Children throw the encased balloons up in the air and try to keep them in the air by batting them with the coat hanger rackets.

This activity provides good exercise for torso muscles and is good for developing balance. Two-year-olds have remarkable success at it because the balloons float down slowly. Children feel powerful.

It is possible to play this game inside. It is ideal for providing some active movement on rainy days.

Riding Toys

Riding toys are wildly popular. Toward the end of the year a two-year-old may be able to master pedaling a tricycle, with great feelings of pride and power. Children not only benefit from the exercise provided by riding toys, but also from the dramatic play potential, as they become motorcycles, trucks and cars in their minds. Can you make a track or road for children to follow on riding toys?

FINE MOTOR DEVELOPMENT

With practice, hand muscles are cooperating with the brain more and more. Simple wooden inlay puzzles, extra-large beads to string, fit-together toys, giant-size pegs and pegboards, give practice for fine-motor control, and are enjoyed by this age.

<u>*Eye-droppers*</u>

Let children transfer colored water from one small container to another using an eye-dropper. They will be gaining skill making their thumb and forefinger work together. Dropping colored water onto white paper towels makes pretty designs.

<u>*Meat Basters*</u>

The "mega" version of the above, meat basters allow children to use the muscles of their whole hand together. Since meat basters in the water table are sometimes used to squirt other children, you might want to set this up as an individual activity, giving the child two small buckets or a two-sided pet feeding dish and invite him to transfer the water from one container to the other using the baster.

Cutting

It is still very difficult for the child to manipulate scissors with success.

<u>*Cutting Play Dough*</u>

Show children how to roll out "snakes" of play dough. Then, using rounded tip scissors, they will enjoy snipping off sections of the snake. This is easy, and it gives practice using the muscles of the hand necessary for cutting. Make sure children are holding scissors correctly when they do this so they are exercising the right muscles. When the "snake" is all cut up, they can squeeze it all together again and roll out a new snake.

In the process, they are getting some practice with another concept, "conservation of matter." That is the idea that the amount of a substance remains the same when it is separated into little pieces. They really won't catch on to this idea for a couple of years yet.

Self-help Skills

The child can feed himself with reasonable success. Adults should not be feeding two-year-olds. Don't be fussy about manners. Do sit at the table and eat with the children so you can provide a model for good manners.

A two-year-old can pull on clothing, although buttoning and snapping are difficult, and tying shoes is a long way off. Especially at this toilet learning period, encourage parents to dress children in clothing the child can handle independently. Let the child do as much as possible for himself, even if it takes longer and doesn't get done exactly right.

Learning to Use the Toilet

This is a social/emotional issue as much as a physical issue. While it's true that a few children can successfully learn to use the toilet in their toddler year, it is more commonly not mastered until the child is nearly three, or later. You can tell the child is ready to begin the process when:

• The child is dry for long periods of time. The child may show facial expressions indicating he is ready to urinate or have a BM.

• The child has the language abilities to follow simple instructions: "Point to your hair," "Sit on the chair," etc., and can talk enough to indicate when he needs to be brought to the bathroom or needs help.

Needless to say, parents and caregivers must work together on the process of teaching the child to use the toilet. Procedures and expectations should be consistent at home and at the child care program. Parents will need to provide lots of underwear and several extra changes of clothes and shoes.

Learning to use the toilet should be low-key and non-punitive. Expect many accidents at first, and from time to time in the next year. Do not try to teach this to a child who is still adjusting to your program or undergoing some stress like illness or a new baby at home.

LANGUAGE DEVELOPMENT

What fun! The child begins the year with a vocabulary of about 200 words, typically, and by the time he's three, generally has command of about 1,000 words or more! He will put together two-, three- and four-word sentences and questions. He will enjoy chanting, repeating syllables over and over in a sing-song way, and generally playing with sounds.

Most of a two-year-old's language is either talking to himself, or directed to an adult. What interchanges there are with other children usually involve the territorial imperative: "MINE!" "Get out!" Remember that children vary widely when they first start talking, and this is not necessarily a reflection on the child's intelligence. Girls often have a slight head start.

Building vocabulary and language skills should be an important subconscious focus of your teaching. Twos are acquiring skill at a dizzying speed. Do not correct mispronunciations, just model the correct way to say it in a later sentence yourself.

Shorthand Language

The first short sentences children come out with leave out all the little words. Sometimes this is called "telegraphic speech" because it sounds like the word-efficient telegraph messages of the old days. "Daddy fix!" "Me go wif."

Pivot Words

This is when a child takes one key word and attaches many other words to it to make different sentences. "Milk all-gone." "Daddy all-gone." "Kids all-gone." You can expand on this idea with many of his words. When a child comes up with a new word, help him combine it with other words.

Some Tips for Stimulating Language Development

- Make your language very clear.
- Be very specific: "Put these red blocks with the other red blocks."
- Look directly at the child when you are talking to him. Watch his eyes and you will know if he is following you or is confused.
- Be aware of the noise level in the room. A high level of noise is detrimental to language development.
- Articulate words clearly. "Let's read that book." "Thank you." "Does the dolly's hat go on her head or on her hand?"
- Match your language to the child's level. With children who have the least productive speech, use simpler words and phrases for things and actions, and increase complexity as the child's language grows. Know where the child is and move forward as he does. Stretch and expand language but don't overwhelm.
- Teach time and space words. Use objects found in the room (blocks, dolls, etc.) to talk about spatial concepts – in front of, behind, over, under, front, back, etc.
- Use objects to talk about comparison – which is bigger, thickest, tallest, etc. Which comes first, second, last. Stimulate comparisons, judgments and evaluations.
- Keep talk and attitudes toward language positive. Use praise, but keep it specific. Keep verbal promises. This helps children learn that adult language can be depended upon.

• Help children learn positive social skills. Teach the magic words of "please" and "thank you" by using these words yourself. Help children express the feelings that they have when someone is rude or kind to them. Model courteous ways of talking with children.

• Use incongruity – make obvious mistakes. As the children develop language skills, make silly mistakes that are obvious. Ask "Is this my (point to your knee) nose?" Kids love silly things.

• Read to children in small groups and individually. Read something every day. Create a comfortable book corner.

• Make up stories to go with pictures.

Poems and Fingerplays

Two-year-olds enjoy simple fingerplays (poems with simple hand movements). They will often not say all the words with you or do all the motions, but they seem to like being part of the process and will join you on the emphasis words, such as the "punch line" of a poem.

Conversations

It will be possible to carry on a simple conversation with a two-year-old. Try to develop the art. Be careful to not only talk "at" children, but to talk "with" them. Listen to what they tell you, and expand upon it. "New shoes." "You got some new pink sneakers! Where did you go to get them?"

One way to have good conversations with a two-year-old is to bring in interesting objects for them to examine and talk about. The food you are having for lunch is always an interesting topic.

A Surprise Bag

Find a special bag that will attract children's attention. A cloth bag, sewn from bright material, with a drawstring, or a gaudy plastic shopping bag would be good. Let children know this is your "Surprise Bag." Every day, bring in some special object in the bag. It could be an exotic item such as a huge shell, or an everyday item like an egg beater. Don't show it to children right away. Put the surprise bag on a shelf and give them time to build suspense and interest. When you take the bag off the shelf, children will automatically gather to see what is in it. Then take the object out of the bag with a bit of drama, and talk about the object with the children. "What is this? Have you ever seen one? Where do you think I got it?

What do you think it is used for?" This is an ideal way to bring in concepts of color, texture, size, weight, etc. By all means, let children handle the object. Concepts become meaningful when children can see, touch, smell and sometimes taste.

Other toys and activities will give you many opportunities to talk to children about what they are doing at the moment and increase their vocabulary and understandings.

When to Test

Generally, if a child is not talking by the age of two-and-a-half, it's probably a good idea to have him tested by an audiologist. The child's pediatrician or the local school can probably recommend someone. Evidence of comprehension is more important than production. If a child can follow directions and point to things you name, there is probably not a problem.

Early Literacy

As with toddlers, your main emphasis is on language development and developing a familiarity and love of books as a source of enjoyment. Although some two-year-olds are beginning to recognize letters because of parental interest, alphabet books, and educational television, it does not have a whole lot to do with learning to read.

When two-year-olds do such things as play with play dough, make lines and patterns with crayons and paint brushes, and sort shells, they are beginning to notice differences in lines and shapes. This ability is necessary later to notice the differences in letter shapes. Location words, "before," "over," etc. are important understandings before children can later make sense of the order of letters and words on a page.

Two-year-olds should not be made to sit down for specific lessons and drills on letters and the sounds they represent. If you really want to grow "eager readers," just read many fine stories and poems to them and work on making them skillful at expressing themselves.

Books

As their language skills increase, simple story books with repeated phrases are fun for two-year-olds. They also enjoy picture books where they can point to objects and name them. Keep a good collection of books for the children. Some will be favorites and can be kept out and available to children at all times. Others you can rotate on the bookshelves. The world of two-year-olds is expanding and they will enjoy books about all kinds of things. Try to see what the children are interested in and find books about those topics. Vehicles of all types are fascinating, and there are many good picture books about them. Animals are also popular. There are some really nice books about "being friends" that could find a lot of use.

Teach children how to handle books properly so that you can leave them out for them to look at whenever they wish. Show children how to put the book on the shelf. Then have the child demonstrate and applaud his success. Show the child how to turn the pages by grasping the edge of the paper rather than pushing the hand across the page. If there is a torn page, let everyone watch while you tape it and repair it and show them again how to turn the page. If the children see that this is a serious matter to you, they will pay attention and learn to handle books well.

COGNITIVE DEVELOPMENT

Cognitive development is closely bound up with progress in the mastery of language and symbols. When the child has words, there is something for his thoughts to hang onto.

Curiosity

How does this work? What's inside? Does this make a noise? Can I take this apart? Can I lift this? Twos have an endless desire to make things work. Turning knobs, flipping switches, playing with locks, etc. all are good fine-motor practice and also have a cognitive component. They are learning about the relationships of spaces and shapes and simple mechanical processes.

The wide world of nature will also give children lots of questions to ask and interesting things to explore. Help them investigate everything from bugs to elephants. Magnifying glasses will further focus their interest. You can find pictures and books about all types of animals and natural objects, but two-year-olds need to see the real thing for these to be really meaningful.

Time

The child of two years has only a vague understanding of time. "Calendar activities" are not appropriate for this age. They do not know what a week is or what a month represents. They are still struggling with yesterday, today, and tomorrow. The names of the days of the week will have very little meaning to them. Although they may memorize them by rote, they will not use them in a meaningful way. Just use the names of the days of the week in your normal conversation. When children are four they will be better able to make sense of them. They do know the difference between night and day.

Number concepts teachers think they are teaching children in calendar activities are really beyond most two-year-olds. Although some can count by rote, numbers do not represent quantities or sequences for children.

Some things you can do to increase a child's understanding of time are:

• Talk about what goes on during the day. Talk about what you will do next. When you are sitting at the snack table, say, for instance, "Soon, when we are through eating we will put our napkins in the wastebasket and wash our hands. Then we will sit in our circle area and hear a story about a baby bear." At lunch talk about what happened that morning. Review. Through these discussions, connected to easily recognizable activities, children are learning the meanings of words such as "soon," "next," "first," "before," etc.

• Talk about what you did yesterday and what will happen tomorrow. Ask children about what they did last night.

• Talk about the weather, especially in connection with words like "today," "yesterday," "last week." You are connecting the passage of time to something more concrete and observable for children.

Yesterday, Today and Tomorrow Project

Carry out some simple activity over three days and talk about yesterday, today and tomorrow in the process. For instance, you might let children paint rocks pink on the first day. On the second day you might say, "Remember, we painted the rocks pink yesterday. Would you like to wash them today? Maybe tomorrow we can paint them green."

One to One Correspondence

The child is likely to show some interest in counting around this age, probably because of adult prompting. More important than rote counting is the idea that one number goes with one thing. Children are often four or older before this idea sinks in. You can, in the meantime, give children play experiences where one thing fits into one space.

- Make parking spaces with room for one toy vehicle in your block area by placing tape strips on the floor.
- Create a stuffed animal storage area using a hanging compartmentalized shoe bag.
- Have the child put one doll in each chair around a play table.

Sorting

When children sort objects, they are making simple "sets" of things that go together – a concept later useful in math learning. At this stage just let them group all sorts of things. Clean-up time gives you ideal opportunities. "Let's put all the things that go in the block corner in this basket, and all the things that go in the housekeeping corner in this basket."

Other ideas:

- Put two colors of napkins in two piles.
- At home, let children help sort clean laundry in piles according to the people the clothes belong to.
- Let children group pictures of different kinds of animals.

Part-Whole Relationships

Who's In There?

Glue a large picture of a familiar character (like Big Bird) inside a file folder. On the cover, cut little doors in strategic places. Let the child open the doors one at a time to reveal parts of the picture underneath, and guess who it is. You can help provide some language. "Who could this be? Let's see...yellow feathers! Who has yellow feathers? What is behind this door? Orange feet!"

In this fun game the child is also getting some practice in deductive reasoning and "part-whole" relationships.

MUSIC

Singing

Simple nursery rhyme melodies, as well as other very simple songs such as "If You're Happy and You Know It..." and "Row, Row, Row Your Boat," are great for two-year-olds. They will be able to follow along with simple melodies, or at least refrains. Repeat the same simple songs over and over. They enjoy the familiar.

Ring Around the Rosy

This familiar game is a traditional favorite of two-year-olds. They enjoy being the "rosy" in the middle. Holding hands and walking around in a circle is also fun, and so is falling down together. Not only are they getting experience with music, they are also gaining pleasure at doing things with someone else, being part of the group.

Jenny's Here Today

This little song is sung to the tune of "Farmer in the Dell." Children sit in a circle and one child at a time jumps up and down in the middle of the circle as the others sing, substituting the name of the child in the middle.

"Jenny's here today,
Jenny's here today,
We all clap together,
'Cause Jenny's here today."

Rhythm Instruments

Making an orderly noise with rhythm instruments gives two-year-olds pleasurable experiences in being part of a group while being conscious of music.

Clapping Variations

With two-year-olds, it's best to start out using the body as the first rhythm instrument. Start with clapping. Have children clap softly, loudly, so you can hardly hear it, etc. Then have them to try to clap just the way you do. Vary the speed and loudness of your clapping. This exercise will make children focus on you, and gain control of their actions.

Then try the same things, patting other parts of the body. "How does it sound when everyone pats their cheeks?" "Let's all pat the top of our heads at the same time." "Now let's rub our hands together. Now stomp our feet." When everybody does the same action at once, it sounds different from when you do it by yourself.

Now try all of these things to recorded music. With you leading, they may get close to the rhythm of the music. Don't make your expectations too high though.

Instruments

It is good if you can start out with children all using the same instrument at one time. Often a program will not have enough of each type of instrument for everyone to have the same thing. Simple homemade rhythm instruments are fine. One easy favorite is to give each child two empty paper towel tubes to hit together. They make a nice, hollow sound. Let them use the instruments in the ways outlined above before adding music.

It's best to keep rhythm activities like these confined to when children are sitting down in a circle, at least at first. Most two-year-olds are not too successful at walking or "marching" to music while playing an instrument. Too many things to do at once.

HOW THEY PLAY

Parallel Play

Toddlers were mostly involved in "solitary play" – everyone doing his own thing, and not paying much attention to what anybody else was doing. Two-year-olds, however, are developing a great interest in other children.

Socially, two-year-olds are "groupies." They really enjoy being near other children. They will often imitate what other children are doing. One girl will run across the room yelling and dive into a pile of pillows. Other children will join her in the identical activity. Although there is not much give and take, they are taking their cues from each other.

This is one reason why simple group activities like looking at a flannel board story or moving together in similar ways to creative movement recordings can find success. "Come over here with us and do what we're doing," is an invitation that may be hard to refuse for a two-year-old.

Chair Train

Two-year-olds seem to love pushing all the chairs in the room together to make a long "train," and then sitting on the chairs and making train (or bus) noises. This is a good match for the age because it's parallel play – they're all doing the same thing, near each other, and they feel powerful moving furniture around.

Dramatic Play

The beginnings of dramatic play were seen in the toddler year when children used objects to represent something else. Two-year-olds add their ability for parallel play to their fantasy play. When children are together in the housekeeping corner, there is not a lot of dialogue and give and take. You are more likely to have three "mommies" taking care of babies than children with family roles assigned.

They enjoy putting on hats, carrying around purses and pretending to cook and care for a baby, all things they have seen many times over. If you have doll highchairs and doll beds, make sure they are large enough and sturdy enough for a child to fit in, because they will surely try. Make sure you do not start sex-role stereotyping at this early stage. Make boys as well as girls welcome in the housekeeping corner. Find props that are as realistic as possible. The more things look like the real thing, the more they will be used.

Children may also pretend to be something else, such as "kitties" or "doggies" crawling around on the floor.

Miniature Play

Little people, small cars, plastic animals and dinosaurs, and sturdy doll house furniture will get the concentrated attention of some children. These can be fun combined with blocks, sand or water. They make the child feel large and powerful. (This kind of toy can be very hard to share.)

Creative Play

Art projects for two-year-olds are largely exercises in learning to use their hands in purposeful ways. Children enjoy the "cause and effect" of art projects – "I move my hand this way, and there is an interesting mark on the paper."

Do not expect two-year-olds to draw pictures that look like something or put together any recognizable project. If a two-year-old comes home with a "bunny" or some such thing, pasted together from various pre-cut pieces of paper, you can be pretty sure that the teacher did most of the process. Very few parents are interested in the level of artistic skill of the teacher!

Scribbling

There is great value in scribbles! First of all, the child is learning to use his two hands for different things simultaneously. He has to hold the paper still with one hand to keep it from sliding around, while making marks with the other hand. Holding onto the crayon and exerting enough pressure to make a mark is another not so easy skill. Eventually, the child notices that the mark changes when he changes the pressure of his hand on the paper. Then he starts to notice the shape of the marks.

A toddler or two-year-old will start out with mostly horizontal zig-zag marks. Then some vertical marks might intersect. Next the child will start making "round and round" continuous circles. Finally comes the closed circle. When the child makes a closed circle, you know it was a conscious, planned thing. Quite an accomplishment, really. But, we are already ahead of ourselves! Circular scribbles don't usually happen before a child is three.

Other Art Activities

Two-year-olds enjoy art activities mainly for their sensory pleasures. Colors are pretty to look at. When a child paints with blue paint, he is more likely to remember what "blue" is. Paste feels good when you spread it around, and smells good too. Finger paint is wonderful and slippery and beautiful designs appear when you move your hands around. Teachers must accept that children will probably taste all of their art materials. That is why art supplies made for young children are non-toxic. Make sure that is true for the materials you use!

Concentrate on offering children many different materials to work with. Find different colors, textures and processes. Don't worry about producing something recognizable. Keep it simple. Some art processes enjoyed by two-year-olds: finger painting, scribbling with crayons, marking pens, chalk; painting at easels with short-handled, wide-tipped brushes; tearing paper and pasting pieces; thing printing.

Don't try to sit a large group of two-year-olds down at a table and have them all do an art activity at once. You'll be asking for disaster, or at least an unsatisfying experience and a big mess. Instead, present activities to two or three children at a time, while other children are occupied in other activities. With a small group, you and the children can relax and talk about what they are doing.

Although children often forget about their art project as soon as they have finished it, parents and grandparents will cherish the masterpieces. Try to save a few before they disintegrate and frame them to send them home to decorate the refrigerator.

Sensory Play

Play materials which involve primarily the sense of touch such as play dough, clay, sand, water, rice, and confetti are a big hit with this age. They just feel good! And they are fun to poke, pour, roll and use other new fine-motor skills.

The Play Environment

The two-year-olds' classroom can be a real transition between the more unstructured environments for infants and toddlers and the structured preschool classroom. Having well-defined "interest centers" will give the children clear cues about what goes where, and what type of play should be going on, helping them develop a sense of order. Group similar activities together and store things close to where they will be used, in well marked containers, so they are easy for children to find and put away again.

A well-developed housekeeping area will encourage their growing dramatic play interest. At first, confine your setting and props to "the house" because these children play roles that are most familiar to them. Dress-up clothes are not as important as props at this age, but they do love hats.

A messy-play area can house both art and sensory play. Locate it near water and over a hard-surface floor that is easy to clean. It's probably best to store art materials out of sight for this age. You can put things out on a table that you want them to use.

A gross-motor area is almost a necessity for this age group which has so much physical energy. Riding toys, a climber, balls and large cardboard blocks go well here. You need a good amount of space for this area.

A fourth section of the room could house table toys – puzzles, manipulatives, blocks, small people and animals, etc. Books could be here, on a separate shelf, or in a special cozy corner with pillows and soft seating.

You don't need to develop a "circle time" area as such because you should not be spending much time with children as a large group. It's much better to settle down with small, informal groups at this age to do short teacher-directed activities.

Going Outside

Twos are the most active age and absolutely need outside time every day that weather permits. If you live where the climate is harsh, plan for when it is best to go outside. Even a few minutes is worth it.

You can do practically everything outside that you would do inside. Dramatic play is especially fun outside. Try hauling out some of your indoor equipment from time to time for this. Add dramatic play components to the sand area. Of course, the major focus outside is gross-motor activity – running, swinging, climbing, riding toys.

SUMMARY

Language is the exciting area of development this year. An appropriate focus for your planning is providing them varied experiences to talk about, and giving them the opportunity to talk.

Give children many opportunities for parallel play, where they can enjoy doing the same thing as other children, near other children. As they play near or with other children, work on teaching them to use words rather than their fists to express frustration.

Moving in different ways and trying out all the different things their bodies can do is an interest that can be accommodated indoors and outdoors, with games, music and equipment, as children develop skills. Plan many activities that will allow twos to practice their developing fine-motor skills.

CHAPTER 5

Three-Year-Olds

THERE IS SUCH A DIFFERENCE between three-year-olds and toddlers. Babyhood has been left behind as the three-year-old child eagerly steps into the wider world. Language is becoming a more and more useful tool for interacting with others, and the child is poised to enjoy learning and social opportunities. Three used to be the age at which traditional nursery schools would enroll children. And with good reason! The child has survived the turbulence of the toddler and twos years and has turned into a generally cooperative little person with a usually sunny disposition. Three-year-olds are generally eager to please and want to do things "right."

SOCIAL EMOTIONAL DEVELOPMENT

Issues of Emotional Development and Self-esteem

Certainly, three-year-olds have and display the full range of emotions. But gradually, through language, they are learning to use words, as well as pure physical outbursts, to express their wants and frustrations.

One thing makes it a bit easier: three-year-olds have not yet learned to hide their feelings. They wear their personality on their sleeves. It's fairly easy to figure out what's going on with a child's emotions. And because they form genuine attachments to teachers and other caring adults, gentle, on the spot coaching can have a real impact for this age.

Relationship to Adults

Even though three-year-olds enjoy the company of other children, they are totally delighted when an adult really plays with them. They thrive on the positive attention of favorite big people, such as the close circle of parents, aunts and uncles, grandparents and other admiring adults who play with them.

Threes are also good at using adults as a resource. They will usually not hesitate to approach an adult to ask for help or to show off something new. Of course, you will be nearby to intercede or help when necessary, but whenever possible, try to teach the child strategies for dealing with a problem by herself. "Go over and tell Kenisha that you don't like it when she grabs things away from you." Then be there to support, help her be heard, help the other child express herself, etc.

Three-year-olds are very susceptible to praise. The over-use of praise by adults can become manipulative. Be genuine in your appreciation of children's efforts, rather than global. Don't praise absolutely everything. Comment on the child's processes if she shows you a painting, for instance. "You used a lot of yellow, didn't you." Or, "I can tell you spent a lot of time on this." Praise the child for things that are really difficult, like waiting or giving someone a turn.

If the child is tired, sad, under stress or not feeling well, she may still climb up on an adult lap and drape herself. The adult is a valuable anchor of safety and security, allowing the child to "refuel" for a few minutes before again facing the world.

Separation

Most preschool children and their parents have trouble saying good-bye from time to time when the parent must leave the scene. As adults, with our well-developed sense of time and knowledge of how the world works and where the other person will be, we have learned to internalize our sadness or anxiety. Young children just cry. It may even seem that for some children, crying at parting is part of the "ritual" they have developed. It is a sign of their attachment to the parent, almost a way of saying, "Don't worry, Mom, you'll always be number one."

Unlike the infants or toddlers who may think they have lost the loved person forever and be totally devastated, the three-year-old can be comforted somewhat by words. First, acknowledge the legitimacy of the child's feelings. Don't brush aside their crying as silly or tiresome. Instead be respectful for what the child is feeling. "It's sad to say good-bye when you wish you could be together all the time." Other children may appear with concerned looks on their faces. You could say, "Samantha is crying because she is sad that her mommy had to leave." You can encourage the other children to figure out ways to comfort the crying child. They may bring a tissue or a blanket, or give their friend a hug.

While this is going on, comfort the child by saying that the parent loves her and left her with you because she knows you will take good care of her and give her fun things to do while she is gone. Also tell the child when the parent will be back. While a three-year-old does not have the ability to tell time, she does have a sense of the order of the day and can mark the passage of time by "events" – elements in your routine. The more familiar she is with your day, the easier this is to do. You can review with her the normal sequence of routines in your day. "In a few minutes we will have snack. Then we will go outside to play. After that we will come inside and have story time. Then we will play. Next it will be lunch time and nap time. After nap time while we are playing inside, your mommy will come back to get you and take you home again."

Pictured Routines

Create a small picture book of the sequence of the routines of your day. Photograph children during all the segments of your day and put one photo for each routine, in order, in a small photo album, one picture per page. Use this book to help children see when their parents will probably be picking them up. This book will be a favorite for children to look through on their own, so leave it in your book corner for them to enjoy.

Pretend to Call

Provide a couple of play telephones. Invite the child to pretend to call the parent at work and tell him or her how she is feeling. You can pick up the other phone and play the part of the parent. "Yes, Mindy, I miss you too. I am at work now and I will come and get you after your rest time today. I love you too...bye." You might suggest that you reverse roles. You play the part of the child and let the child pretend to be the absent parent.

I'll Be Back!

Later you might encourage this child to play out the situation in dramatic play using a doll. Let the child be the parent who is dropping off the doll in child care. You or another child could play the part of the adult caregiver. This allows the child to put herself in a situation of power. Rather than "opening the wound," it can help the child gain some better understanding of the situation.

Fears

It is common for three- and four-year-olds to develop fears. Loud noises, animals, strange people or costumed characters may arouse anxiety in some children. They may be afraid to go to bed at night because of the "monsters" that MIGHT materialize under the bed. Some parents have wondered, "How could this child, who has been so loved and sheltered, be so frightened by imagined dangers?" The child's basic temperament has some influence. The basically cautious or fearful child may become more so at this time. However, you might see the bold, adventurous child affected by imagined threats as well.

While we can and should stay away from scary or highly adventurous stories and shield children from frightening characters, you cannot totally prevent their anxiety. It's as though they are developing a sense of menace. More aware of the world outside the family, these children are beginning to feel how vulnerable they really are, and are sorting out what is really dangerous and what is not. While not all three-year-olds develop obvious fears, many become cautious in general.

Children's fears should be taken seriously, not laughed at or brushed aside. Even if we, the adults, know the clown is harmless, the fear is real for the child. Let the child hang onto you, while you say reassuring things and allow the child to approach the new situation when she is ready. When the child senses you are "there" for her, she will be more able to come to terms with what she is afraid of.

<u>*Puppet with a Problem*</u>

Your "pet puppet" could bring up a problem with the children, and admit with some embarrassment that he is afraid of the dark (or some other issue you know a particular child might be battling). The puppet could ask the group if any of them have ever felt that way and what they do about it. Chances are, the children will have some very useful advice for the puppet. This serves a couple of purposes. It helps children feel they are not alone in their fears. It also empowers them when they give advice to someone else. You could help them along by asking questions such as, "What else could he do?" "Does anyone use a night light?" You could also make a list of the children's advice and post it on the wall or include it in a parent newsletter.

We will continue to discuss this in the next chapter for children who are a bit more verbal and have well-developed imaginations.

Imaginary Friends

Imaginary friends are not uncommon with this age. While not all children invent these companions, it's estimated that a third to a half of children seem to conjure up a pretend personality that can take the blame for misdeeds as well as provide company. It shows that the child is developing imagination and can create mental images, rather than being anchored in the literal here and now, as was the case for two-year-olds. The three-year-old is developing a conscience and is beginning to know the difference between right and wrong. Since the child wants so much to please adults, an imaginary companion to blame things on is a convenient tool. Generally, it's advisable for the adults to play along without making too much of it. If Georgie makes a mess, make the child clean it up, saying, "You'll have to talk to Georgie about this and make sure he doesn't do it again." But you don't have to go so far as to set another place at the table. The child can create other accommodations for her friend in her imagination. Don't worry that this is abnormal in any way. Children with an imaginary friend are creative and may be less bored than other children.

Dangerous Wishes

There is a mix of reality and fantasy in the thinking of young children. The world still has a lot of magic in it. Children might think that something they dreamed really happened. They might also believe that wishing for something hard enough can make it happen. This causes fear and guilt when bad things really do happen and the poor child thinks she made it happen because she had a bad wish. Mr. Rogers' song, "Scary, Bad Wishes Don't Make Things Come True" addresses this issue. A child can benefit from reassurance from a trusted adult that she did not cause something to happen.

Relationships with Other Children

Three-year-olds are the "social butterflies" of the preschool set. They love having friends and are often very affectionate with them. You will often see three-year-olds holding hands, or sitting with their arms around each other. Their evolved language skill allows them to interact with peers more than two-year-olds did, smoothing social give and take. This is the really exciting development of the year! They are gaining an awareness that other people are "real" and have feelings and rights. Friendships blossom with three-year-olds. Many children develop a special friend whom they seek out in play situations.

Developing Friendships

Children under three form social attachments by imitating each other. (See previous chapter.) Three-year-olds do this too and you'll see much spontaneous imitation in movements and sounds to establish social contact. Now, also using words, three- and four-year-olds will use "Me too!" to further establish similarities. You can play a game about likes and dislikes. "Who likes macaroni and cheese?" "Who likes kitties?"

While three-year-olds love having friends, to a certain degree, a "friend" to a three-year-old is someone who is playing with you right now. Someone with interesting toys or good ideas. That's why when conflict occurs, one so often hears, "You're not my friend anymore!" Sometimes children need help in learning how to play with others. Although all three-year-olds are interested in playing with others and being "friends," some are more skillful than others. Children who have had more group experiences, and those who have had the chance to play with older children and siblings, often have better developed social skills.

Three-year-olds, with their new focus on friendships, can sometimes be seen excluding other children from a play situation. "You can't play here. Just Joe and me can play here, right Joe?" This, of course, is painful for the excluded child, as well as for adults watching. Sometimes you can ease the situation by suggesting an interesting role for the excluded child. "It looks like this family needs a big brother..."

A group of three-year-olds does not usually have the strong hierarchy of older groups of children. "Leadership" will shift from moment to moment depending on who has a good idea. Still, natural leaders or "popular" children sometimes emerge. These are often attractive children or ones who are generally fun to be with. The flip side is that certain children may be consistently shunned by the other children. It is very important to try to figure out what is going on and intervene. Often you will see a play pattern emerge that needs correcting. Perhaps the child is overly aggressive, shoving the other children and grabbing toys. Another child may be overly bossy and insist on doing everything her way. It is important to help the child figure out better ways to play because if uncorrected, these negative patterns may be strengthened and children will shun them more until they become "loners" in later years. Interacting with peers is important for effective learning, so there are intellectual as well as social consequences.

Social Graces

It is endearing to see how three-year-olds can master some of the social graces. "Please," and "thank you," and "let's" are commonly heard, especially if they have good adult models. Naturally, you will model the use of polite conventions yourself, saying "please," and "thank you" in the course of normal interactions with the child. A gentle suggestion or reminder, without embarrassing the child, is also appropriate. You could whisper to the child, "Don't forget to say 'Thank you' to Aunt Martha."

Thank-you Notes

When you have had a special visitor, or someone has bestowed a favor or present on the child, encourage her to decorate a piece of paper with crayons or paint, and take dictation from her about what she would like to say to that person. Read it back, and involve her in mailing the note.

Sense of Humor

"Slapstick" humor is popular. Three-year-olds like to laugh at the ridiculous. Accidents will seem funny. They know enough about the world to know how things are supposed to be and look. Variations will interest them. At this point they will laugh both at others and themselves. They also enjoy pronouncing words in silly ways and hearing nonsense rhymes and other word games. Children enjoy being clowns. Wild, silly gross-motor activities have great appeal. Movement and music activities can feed this interest.

Typical Behavior Issues

It is still difficult for children to realize that someone else has a different point of view. It is only through lots of practice and social give and take that they learn to put themselves in someone else's shoes. Plan lots of activities that are more fun to do with someone else than alone and children will learn the benefit of giving way occasionally and cooperating with other children.

Words are gaining power. Children are beginning to be able to come up with solutions to problems with other children. Encourage a child to use words instead of physical aggression. At first you may have to model words for them to parrot. "Janie, instead of screaming and hitting, say, 'No! I have that now. You can have it when I'm done.'" "Marcia, do you hear Janie? She said you can have it when she's done in a few minutes. She doesn't like it when you grab."

Three-year-olds can be obstinate, and may stand like a rock and simply refuse to do something. Try some gentle, positive suggestion techniques and try to avoid confrontations. "Let's do this...," or "How about we..." are good phrases to employ when you want a child's cooperation.

Knowing their eagerness to please adults and their susceptibility to praise, using "positive reinforcement" can have good effects. Catch a child doing something right and notice it out loud. "Laura, you did a good job using words to tell Sean you were mad."

Three-year-olds are less likely than two-year-olds to have a kicking, screaming all-out tantrum. When they still resort to tantrums, often it is because they have learned to use this as an effective tool to manipulate adults to comply with their wishes. Don't let them succeed. Recognize and accept their feelings. "I know, you're angry because you can't have that now. When you are through making all this noise we can talk about it. In the meantime we'll be over there playing."

Sometimes an otherwise agreeable three-year-old goes through a difficult stage at about three-and-a-half. It can be a time of testing, and rebelling. With patience and gentle firmness on your part, the child usually returns to her pleasant self by the time she's four.

Anticipate and Rehearse

Everybody feels more comfortable in a strange situation if they have had a little "rehearsal" about what is going to happen and how they are to behave. Whether it's going out to eat with the family, going for a walk in the neighborhood, or visiting the library for a storytime, some advance practice can build success. Since threes are getting good at pretend play, it can be fun.

For instance, if you have a very casual reading style with children, allowing them to climb on your lap and drape themselves over you, and you're going to the library where things may be a little more formal, it could be fun to make a game of it. "Let's pretend we're going to the library and I'm the library lady." Tell them how they will be expected to behave, let them act it out and clap and praise when they do it correctly. Then congratulate them when they succeed at the real thing. For everyday situations that may be hard to remember, you could state the rule beforehand and have the children repeat the rule. Also repeat why the rule is important.

Taking Turns

Three-year-olds quarrel over possessions more than anything else. Snatching a toy and running away with it is typical of both boys and girls. Taking turns is a new concept and they'll need help in understanding it. They are starting to be able to wait a short time for what they want. With their strong desire for friendship, they are learning that you give a little, you get a little. It does take experience with other children to learn to take turns. This is a skill that is developed through practice – positive, successful experiences. Adults will have to guide children in the process. Help children with the dialogue and follow through:

"Jennifer, say, 'May I have a turn riding the trike?'"

"Donna, let Jennifer know when you are through riding in a few minutes, okay?"

Giving the child with the desired toy some control of when to turn it over is usually a good idea. Often, she will do it quite reasonably if she feels she can decide when. You also need to teach a child what to say when she is not ready to turn over the desired item. "Don't take my toy because I'm still playing with it."

Sometimes, after a reasonable amount of time, the child will need some gentle nudging. When you suggest it may be time to turn the desired item over to someone new, it may help to have an interesting alternative activity ready for the child who is relinquishing the turn. "Donna, if you are ready to let Jennifer have the trike, you can come over here and play with Joshua and me. We're painting the building with water."

Let's Pretend to Take Turns

It might even be fun to do a pretend game about taking turns. Suggest to children whom you know are just learning this skill, "Let's pretend you two wanted to take turns playing with this truck (or whatever)." Then coach them through it. "Jamal, you start being the one playing with the truck. Okay, Alicia, pretend you want a turn. What will you say to Jamal?"

If needed give some words. "Can you say, 'Hey there, old buddy, Jamal...could I have a turn with that when you're done?'" "Now, what do you say, Jamal?" If needed you can supply some fun words for him too: "Why Alicia, my good friend, I'd be happy to give you a turn." Adding a little humor makes this less like a lecture.

Give Reasons

It's respectful as well as instructive to tell children why a behavior is not allowed. You sound less bossy and the child starts learning about safety and may be able to regulate herself more easily in the future.

"No climbing on the fence because the fence has splinters and you might get hurt."

"Don't push Jordan off the tricycle because that will make him mad and he won't want to share with you. Instead, here is what you can say to him..."

"Throwing sand is not allowed because it might get in someone's eyes and that hurts a lot."

Aggression

While three-year-olds often act out in aggressive ways more to explore what this might feel like than to express real hostility toward other children, there can be times when children will kick, bite, scratch, hit and hurt their playmates. This needs quick and immediate attention from the supervising adult. One rule can cover it all: "No hurting others."

GROSS MOTOR DEVELOPMENT

The child's growth is starting to level off now. At three it is said that a child has reached half of her adult height. Proportions are changing. The child's legs grow faster than the rest of her and she is losing that top-heavy look of infancy and toddlerhood. The three-year-olds have become quite graceful compared to two-year-olds, and they no longer lead with their tummies. Instead of holding their arms out to the side for balance, they swing their arms easily at their sides and walk with sureness.

Coordination is developing. Three-year-olds are capable of a wide variety of movements. Running seems to be a joy. So is galloping, jumping and "dancing" to music. In fact, threes, with their new fluency of movement, like to try all kinds of actions.

This is an ideal time to introduce some "creative movement" activities. Since three-year-olds are newly social, they will enjoy doing movement activities in small or large groups. Possibilities are endless. Because of their social nature and their "humor of the absurd" they especially enjoy silly or funny movements. They'll have fun with circle games like "Here We Go Looby-Loo," and enjoy participating with the many children's music recordings that involve movement. Follow-the-leader games also let them practice many movements.

Climbing

Three-year-olds usually alternate feet when they climb up stairs. They may still walk down stairs one step at a time, not alternating feet. A sturdy climbing apparatus inside as well as outside will still be very much enjoyed.

Balance Beam

Since most three-year-olds no longer have that wide stance and their balance is much more refined than a year ago, a low wide board to walk along presents a challenge they enjoy. A simple two-by-four, about four feet long, placed directly on the floor will do. Or you may find more success at first with a plank that is six or eight inches wide. Do balance beam activities in a small group of four or five children while other children are doing something else so nobody has to wait too long for a turn.

Walk the Plank

Try some of the following motions. At first they may want to hold your hand for security and a little help with their balance.

- *Walk forward across the board.*
- *Walk sideways across the board.*
- *Walk backward across the board.*
- *Walk across the board, on all fours, touching the board with hands as well.*
- *Tip-toe across the board, forward and backward.*

Tricycles

This is the "year of the tricycle!" Some two-year-olds can master a tricycle, but most often it's not accomplished until the child is three. A child will typically first propel the tricycle by pushing along with feet on the ground like she did with the wheeled riding toys popular with toddlers and two-year-olds. What a proud accomplishment when she figures out how to use the pedals! Do make sure the tricycle is the right size so that the child can reach the pedals. Since very few child care or preschool programs have one tricycle for each child, the much wanted tricycles will also give children practice in the fine art of taking turns! A tricycle usually becomes a car, a fire engine, or a motorcycle in the child's mind, making it a prime tool for dramatic play and the exercise of the imagination. If you doubt that, just listen to the sound effects! You can add props such as hats and pieces of garden hose to your outside area to encourage this extension of the play.

Throwing and Ball Play

Children are gaining some basic skill at rolling and bouncing balls, if they have a chance to practice. Catching a ball is still quite difficult, although the child will have occasional success. A good circle game is to bounce or roll the ball to each other.

Bean bags offer a little more control than balls and activities such as passing the bean bag around the circle and balancing it on various parts of the body give good practice. Threes also greatly enjoy throwing bean bags at a simple target with holes in it. Bean bags may be a bit easier to catch than balls.

FINE MOTOR DEVELOPMENT

The muscles of the hand are beginning to do what the brain tells them to, but they still have a long way to go. For instance, holding a pencil is still very difficult. Three-year-olds will often hold a pencil, crayon or paint brush with their whole fist.

Sensory materials like play dough, clay, water and sand are very popular with three-year-olds, and allow them to practice using their hands in controlled ways. Squeezing, poking and rolling build hand muscle strength. Pouring requires coordination. All of these activities, while providing hand muscle practice, also stretch the imagination as the materials take on different shapes.

"Fingerplays," poems and songs with accompanying hand motions, also provide some hand muscle practice. It is something three-year-olds enjoy doing together. *Wee Sing – Children's Songs and Fingerplays*, by Pamela Conn Beall and Susan Hagen Nipp, is one of the many good resources containing familiar rhymes available to parents and teachers.

Stringing Beads

Stringing extra-large wooden or plastic beads is fun for three-year-olds. Stiffen the ends of the strings with glue or tape. Thin plastic tubing is also good for stringing large beads. Threes will also enjoy stringing O-shaped cereal into necklaces. Make a collection of other hollow objects, such as spools, hair curlers, plastic straws cut into pieces and napkin rings for them to string onto tubing or yarn.

Construction Toys

Fit-together toys, such as plastic bricks and their many variations, offer just the right challenge. The child has to line up the pieces correctly and exert pressure. Many other concepts are learned through these toys as well, such as length, shape and size.

Art Activities

Art activities are a great way for children to practice their fine-motor skills and develop their creativity at the same time. Three-year-olds enjoy the whole range of traditional preschool art activities such as finger painting, brush painting, coloring and scribbling, pasting, gluing, printing and cutting. (See below under *Creative Play,* page 125.)

Cutting

This is the year children usually learn to cut with scissors. Because it is a new skill, it is often very popular. For children who still find cutting difficult, try letting them cut play dough "snakes" as described in the last chapter. This is easy, satisfying and gives them practice moving their hand muscles in the right way.

It's a good idea to have a "cutting table" set up and available to children most of the time. They start by successfully cutting "fringes" around the edges of the paper. Later they will be able to cut all the way across a piece of paper. Cutting on a line, moving the paper with the other hand, and cutting out pictures from magazines comes next. If you have paste and paper handy, the cutting experience will be expanded.

Although a dominant hand is not always evident at this age, if a child shows great difficulty learning to cut, you might try offering "lefty" scissors. New scissors available for young children can be used successfully with either hand.

A caution – although paper can be difficult to learn to cut, hair seems amazingly easy, and sometimes impossible to resist. Supervise cutting activities closely with three-year-olds.

Thumb and forefinger pressed together exercise the "pincer muscle." In addition to cutting, activities such as peeling hard boiled eggs and sorting beans into egg carton compartments give good practice. The following activity also uses these muscles and will hold children's attention for a long time as they learn more about colors, creating new ones of their very own.

Eye-dropper Color Transfer

Fill an ice cube tray with water. Put red food coloring in a compartment at one end, yellow in the middle, and blue at the opposite end. Keep the others clear. Show the child how to transfer color from one compartment to another using an eye-dropper. After the child has made all the beautiful colors, she can drop them onto white paper towels or coffee filters to have a permanent record to take home.

SELF-HELP SKILLS

It is especially in the self-help routines that we see that three-year-olds are no longer babies. As the child gains skill in attending to daily routines, her sense of independence and self-esteem also grows.

Bathroom Time

Most three-year-olds can ask to go to the bathroom. (See Chapter Four for a discussion on learning to use the toilet.) Children are usually able to pull their own pants down and up again and manage easy zippers and buttons. Some clothing such as overalls may require help. You may wish to encourage parents to dress children in clothing they can handle themselves, not so much to save the teacher time, but to allow the child to grow in independence. Even though children are capable of going to the bathroom independently, this activity still needs adult supervision. Expect accidents from time to time.

Handwashing

Three-year-olds are quite capable of washing their own hands. Show them how to work the faucets (make sure they can reach them), how to use the soap dispenser, get the paper towels and dispose of the towel.

Make handwashing an integral, automatic part of the child's routine after going to the bathroom, after blowing their noses, and before eating.

<u>*Soap Gloves*</u>

To encourage children to scrub their hands thoroughly, show them how to make "gloves" from soap lather.

Eating

Children are very capable of feeding themselves at this age. Do not feed children. Do not be fussy about table manners and neatness, and treat accidents casually. Children can serve themselves most foods if you show them how. Although it may be more efficient to dish out food for children, allowing them to help themselves from small serving dishes and pass dishes around gives them a new social skill. They can also learn to scrape their plates and put their plates on a stack. If the adult sets a good model for children, manners will come in time.

Dressing

You can expect children to be able to put on their own jackets or coats to go outside. If they do not yet know how, teach them the following technique:

<u>*The Old Coat Trick*</u>

Place the child's coat on the floor with the neck at her feet, inside up. The child stoops down and puts each hand in one of the sleeves. She then picks up the coat and flips it over her head, slipping her arms into the sleeves.

They may need help buttoning or getting a zipper started, but can unbutton and unzip easily. Children have been able to take off shoes and socks since toddlerhood! At three they can put their socks back on themselves, and can get their shoes on their feet (not necessarily the right ones) but will need help tying shoes.

Let Them Help

Cooperative little people that they are, most three-year-olds love to help in daily classroom and home routines. Some things three-year-olds can help with, when shown how, are:

- Setting the table
- Passing out snacks
- Folding cot sheets
- Putting away nap mats or cots
- Straightening books on the book shelf
- Watering the plants
- Feeding the classroom pet
- Wiping off the table after meals
- Putting away toys when it is time to clean up

It is true that an adult can probably accomplish all of these things more quickly working alone than with the benefit of three-year-old helpers. However, speed is not the objective. Allowing children to help makes them feel needed and important, and builds skill in these routines in the process.

LANGUAGE DEVELOPMENT

Most three-year-olds seem to talk all the time. Fluent talk is a new "emerging skill" for children. They are driven to practice all the new sounds and combinations they can make over and over, adding new ones all the time. Although some three-year-olds have trouble pronouncing all the sounds of the language, they can generally say what they want to say and have basic grammatical structures mastered. Most children who are "late talkers" are spouting forth by the time they are three-and-a-half.

It is not uncommon for three-year-olds to stutter a little when going through that difficult time at three-and-a-half. As a rule, the less attention paid to a child's stammering, the sooner it disappears. Try to wait patiently for the child to get the words out rather than interrupting and supplying the words.

Some parents are anxious about a child's frequent mispronunciations. Some three-year-olds articulate very clearly, while others persist in substituting sounds, although most are still understandable. Again, it's best to relax and wait. Pronunciation will probably clear up by itself within the next year, especially if the child is surrounded by good language models in adults.

For the first time, children direct speech as much at other children as at adults. Their ability to express themselves adequately in most situations is one reason for the blooming of social relationships with other children.

Conversing

At first, much of the talk that children direct at each other is in the form of directives – "Stop that!" or possessives – "Mine!" If you listen to two three-year-olds "conversing" it can be quite comical. Often it is a "dual monologue" with both children talking about their own topic, not relating much to what the other child is saying. It's as though they're going through the motions of having a conversation, imitating adult behavior they have seen, but not quite connecting. This improves as the year goes on and they have more shared experiences.

Unfortunately, studies have shown that there is very little conversation between teachers and children in some child care programs. The adults mostly speak *at* the children, giving directions and prohibitions, rather than conversing *with* children. Make it a point to have a conversation with each child individually during the day. See how many "turns" back and forth you can reach. In order to encourage children to converse, avoid using only "yes" and "no" questions like, "Did you eat cereal for breakfast today?" Instead, try to ask a content question like, "What do you think is going on in this picture?" Model good conversation skills when you are eating snack and lunch – natural social situations. Talk about what the child is doing at the moment, and things present in the environment. Expand on what the child says. If she points and says, "Truck," you can say, "Yes, that's a red pickup truck. Where do you think it's going?" Try to follow the child's interest.

Vocabulary Development

Three-year-olds love new words and they're adding new ones every day. The average three-and-a-half-year-old has more than 1,200 words in her active vocabulary and many more that she understands in context. It's important to keep in mind that children understand a great many more words than they actually speak. Some of their favorites are "secret," "surprise," "new," and "different."

Children learn new words by hearing them in a meaningful context. The best way to increase their vocabulary is to surround them with rich language experiences. Bring in interesting things for children to look at and talk about. Most of all, talk about things they can see or experience right then and there. Notice the weather, the loud truck on the road, the color of someone's new shoes.

Three-year-olds can usually understand the space words, such as: on, under, beside, between, back, corner, over, from, by, up, on top of, downstairs, outside. To strengthen their understanding, here are two fun activities:

Follow the String

Take a long piece of string or yarn around your room, taping it down every so often to hold it in place. Make it go behind, under, over and through objects. Then have children, one at a time, follow the path of the string around the room. While the child does this, you be the "announcer" and describe with great flourish where the child is: "Caleb is crawling under *the table. Now he is climbing* up *the steps. Now,* down *the steps. Now he is going* through *the tunnel, and there he goes* over *the chair. Now he is* next to *the drinking fountain, and here he comes* back *to us!" Then have everybody clap. You may have to have another adult or older child do this first to give them the idea while you describe the actions. When children have done this activity many times, see if they can take turns being the "announcer," telling where someone else is. You might even produce a pretend microphone for them.*

Puppet Directions

Children love to perform for a puppet. Have a puppet tell children to do various things involving location words. "Put the block in the suitcase." "Put the ball behind the chair." "Hold the doll upside down," etc. What might be boring to do for the parent or caregiver will be fun to do for the puppet.

Action words and descriptive words are added to children's speech, along with names of things, as children hear them used in meaningful ways. A puppet could give children different actions to do, or ask them to find things of a particular description.

Early Literacy

The best pre-reading exercise you can offer children is simply to read to them often, and with obvious enjoyment. Three-year-olds can learn to recognize shapes, sizes and colors. They can usually recognize most upper-case letters, but if they don't, don't worry. It's okay to introduce these concepts if you don't "push" them and drill children. Keep it light. They have time.

Reading books out loud to children is one of the most important things you can do. You are providing several things:

• Pleasure. You are presenting books as a means for enjoyment. A passion for books and reading is one of the most valuable gifts adults can give children.

• Vocabulary development. Three-year-olds enjoy new words. Through stories, they will hear new words in a meaningful context and absorb the meanings.

• Listening skills. Starting with simple picture books and getting more complex as the year progresses, children will develop the skill to follow the simple line of a story. Their attention span will increase with experience.

• Stretching imagination. Books take children out of their immediate environment and into the realm of their imagination.

• Talk written down. As children see a parent or teacher run his or her finger over the words as she reads, they slowly get the idea that those little black squiggles represent sounds and words, a necessary pre-reading awareness.

What Type of Books?

Three-year-olds are gradually moving beyond the earlier "word books" (books with a picture and a matching word). Now they like simple stories about things that are comfortable and familiar, as opposed to scary and exciting (more to the taste of four-year-olds). Stories about everyday life, families, the farm, and transportation catch their interest. Books with animal characters are especially popular. They make a familiar situation different enough to be interesting.

In addition to reading at your story time, make books available for children to look through on their own. It's nice if an adult can make herself available to read to a small group of children during the general play time.

Hints on Reading to a Group

- Size of the group. The fewer children there are in the group, the easier it will be for children to concentrate. When possible, arrange to read to just a few children at a time. When they can snuggle next to you and see you trace your finger over the words while they look at the picture, the enjoyment of a story is greatly increased. If there are too many children in the group it will be too difficult for them to see the pictures and not get distracted by other children. If reading time becomes a battle of getting children to sit still, stop wiggling and kicking, children may begin to view reading as a negative experience.
- Timing. *When* you decide to read to children will make a difference in their ability to listen and enjoy the story. If children are tired or anxious, have been working or playing quietly for a relatively long time, they may need to do a bit of active moving first. If children have been playing actively outside it may take a few "calming activities" to get them ready to sit quietly. Many teachers find several times in their routines when a story is just the right thing. In the morning group time it pulls children together and starts the day on a pleasant note. The right story can be calming before nap time. Late afternoon when toys have been put away is another time books have been helpful. Children can relax and listen and don't have to interact with others.

- Distractions. It can be difficult to hold children's attention when they can see other children engaged in exciting activities outside or in other parts of the environment. Arrange yourself so their line of sight does not have other distractions. Parents coming in to get children in the middle of a story can also shatter the concentration of the other children. Perhaps you could request in a newsletter or other communication to parents that they wait a few minutes until the end of the story when they arrive at that time.
- Set the stage. Sometimes it doesn't work well to simply launch into a story once you have gathered children. Try catching their attention with a related object. For instance, finish sewing on a button to a piece of clothing as children watch. Then tell them you know a story about a teddy bear who lost his button, and then take out the *Corduroy* book.
- Voice. Keep your voice in a comfortable middle range and be sure you speak loudly enough so all the children can hear you. Change your voice for the different characters in the book to give them more life.
- Pace. Most people who read out loud to children make the mistake of reading too fast. When you read quickly your voice cannot be as expressive, and take on different voices for different characters. Learn to pause occasionally to add emphasis.
- Book selection. Always pre-read any book you are going to read to your group. Make sure it is a book you like to read. If you are bored by a book, this will be transmitted to the children. Judge the vocabulary. It is okay to read books slightly above the level of children. You may want to change some of the words, or shorten the story.

Extend the Stories

It's always fun to make a book come alive by doing something related to the topic of the book. Here are some possibilities:

• Do something that happened in the book. After reading *The Little Red Hen* you might bake bread.

• Find objects or costumes related to things in the story that children can play with afterwards, such as a red hooded cape and a basket for *Little Red Riding Hood.*

• Create a flannel board story based on the book. Flannel board figures can be made of felt or flannel. You can also cut out copies of paper pictures and back them with felt to use on the flannel board. When telling the story, you could ask children to hold certain characters until it is their turn in the story.

• Act out the story. Children who are very familiar with favorite stories will have fun acting them out with the "directing" of adults. Such stories as "Caps for Sale," by Esphyr Slobodkina work very well for this.

• Have a snack related to a food in the book. Gingerbread cookies for *The Gingerbread Man* or oatmeal (porridge) for *The Three Bears.*

Have Books Available

Make sure your environment has many beautiful books for children to explore on their own as well as in the cozy company of an adult. An inviting "library corner" with comfortable seating or pillows and good lighting is a standard in early childhood classrooms. Also think of other places to put picture books. The dramatic play area is a natural. Children can often be seen pretending to read, turning the pages of a book and pointing to the words. Dolls and teddy bears make ideal friends for a child to read to. When a child "reads" pictures in a book there are many carry-overs to actual reading. Pictures are symbols, after all. Letters and words are simply more abstract symbols. If a child learns to use one kind of symbol, the ability to use others will come more easily.

Poetry

Don't forget poetry. With their new facility with language, three-year-olds will enjoy learning simple poems and songs. It can make them feel as if they are mastering the words and can play with them.

Fingerplays are simple poems accompanied by hand and body movements. These, as well as Mother Goose rhymes, are greatly enjoyed by three-year-olds. They enjoy doing the same action as everyone else, being part of the group.

"Circle Time"

Three-year-olds are ready to enjoy simple "circle time" activities, if you are in a group child care setting, but be sure to keep your time short and fun – not more than ten or fifteen minutes. The main benefit of a large group activity is to get children used to gathering together and having a feeling of belonging. Develop a few rituals to make it easier. Always meet at the same time in your daily schedule, and in the same place. You might always start with a particular song. Singing and moving to music are good group activities. A puppet can tell children what's going to happen that day. You might have a "surprise bag" as described in the chapter on two-year-olds – always a popular draw.

Remember that most activities that people routinely do at "circle time" can be done as well or better with a small group or individually. So, keep it to three or four short activities. You want it to be fun and low-stress. If children resist coming to your circle time, you may be dragging it on too long.

COGNITIVE DEVELOPMENT

Language development has a huge impact on cognitive development. Cognitive development involves "thinking skills" that help the child organize the world and develop the ability later on for abstract thinking and using symbols. Words are symbols in themselves – they are sounds that represent something else. The more words a child knows, the more she is able to think about things not present. Language makes it easier to think. Pre-verbal children just act and react to what happens around them. Once children have language, you can begin to reason with them.

Children make a big jump in their ability for pretend play in this year because they can use language to describe what they are doing and have conversations with other players, and because they can use objects to represent something else. Whole new worlds of fantasy open up. See the "How They Play" section below for a further discussion.

Although parents and teachers of younger groups surely have touched on them, this is a good year to start focusing on the traditional "academic" concepts of color, shape and size. Try to do this by building concepts into art activities or simple games you present and normal conversations, rather than isolated "lessons." What you are really doing is strengthening children's vocabulary to include descriptive words that help them organize their thoughts.

Colors

Colors are really quite an abstract. That's why they're difficult for children until they suddenly "get it." Colors present a way of describing and ordering our world. Routinely use color words to describe things during the day – children's clothing, chairs, flowers, etc. (In truth, in our color-conscious world, it is rare that children do not pick up color concepts in their day-to-day language learning before they reach school-age.)

Teachers have thought of many fun ways to teach colors:

- Color card matching games are easy to make.
- Glue circles of different colors of paper in the bottoms of muffin tin cups, and let children put matching large wooden beads or balls in the cups.
- Children can cut out magazine pictures of certain colors and paste them on a large sheet of paper to make a "color poster."
- Try having a "color week" in which you concentrate on one color all week. Use that color of paint at the easel, make food of that color, invite parents to dress children in that color, or have bandannas of that color for children to wear.
- Let children sort socks by color.
- Art activities of all types present real experiences with colors.

Shapes

Shapes are part of our world. There are many ways to point them out to children. Many preschool toys, of course, focus on shapes that you can talk about with children. Learning to recognize and name shapes is a pre-reading skill. Teachers will talk about shapes when they teach children to print letters.

- Have a puppet bring out a collection of items from a suitcase, all of a certain shape.
- Draw large shapes on the sidewalk or concrete area for children to walk around.
- Arrange chairs in certain shapes to play "Simplified Musical Chairs" (see music activity on page 121).
- Find children's picture books that focus on shapes.

• Shape collages – Let children make random designs by pasting or gluing an assortment of precut shapes.

• Go on a "triangle" hunt or a "circle hunt" around the building and see how many objects of that shape children can find. You can "plant" certain shapes for them to discover.

Volume

To understand mathematics, children will need to understand full, empty, half, large, small, etc. Most three-year-olds do not comprehend that short, wide containers can hold the same volume as tall, thin containers, or that a round ball of play dough will contain the same amount of play dough when it is flattened into a pancake. And you can't teach them this! They eventually figure it out themselves, through much playing and experimenting with materials.

Give them lots of opportunity to play with sand and water, and choose containers for them to fill and pour from that have different shapes, but similar volumes.

Play dough and various kinds of clay give children experiences with solid substances. Add a simple balance scale to the play dough table, as well as various containers for them to put the dough in, plastic knives to cut the play dough into several pieces, a small rolling pin with which to flatten it, etc.

Part-Whole Relationships

This is a perception skill. Children need to be able to see the components of a larger picture to later see individual letters in a word, or words in a sentence. Puzzles are among the best ways to let children experience part-whole relationships. They also gain fine-motor skill in the process of putting puzzle pieces together. Three-year-olds can typically do a three or four piece inlay puzzle, where pieces combine to make one large picture. As the year progresses and they gain experience they will advance much farther, so it's good to have puzzles of increasing difficulty.

Homemade Puzzles

Let the child help you create your own puzzles from magazine pictures, or even better, calendar pages. The child could find the pictures that interest her. Glue the picture to thin cardboard and laminate them or encase in clear contact paper. Cut into several pieces. The child can help you decide where to make the cuts.

Classifying

Sorting activities of all types are fun and useful for three-year-olds. As they classify objects by attributes (large/small, round/square, heavy/light) they are noticing details about things, and are also thinking about the way things can be the same or different. You could have different things available to sort every week. Find interesting containers to put them in to make it even more fun. Lots of sorting activities present themselves in everyday tasks – putting dishes away, putting clothes in stacks according to whom they belong, placing silverware back in a compartmentalized drawer, etc.

Symbols

Children this age can also learn to recognize letters and numbers, and can recite the alphabet and do some rote counting. Follow their interest, but don't press these things too much; they still have plenty of time.

Let children use other types of symbols as well. Pictures are symbols. Picture books without words are particularly good. Also let children talk about what is going on in pictures you have cut from magazines.

Let children find other symbols in their world, such as stop signs and stop lights, exit signs, a red cross on a first aid kit, and the skull and crossbones poison sign. Ask children, "What does this symbol mean?"

Time Words

Three-year-olds live very much in the "here and now." They don't plan for tomorrow or reflect much on the past. Abstract concepts of time are quite difficult for three-year-olds. One reason is that they cannot "see" time. They do have many time words in their vocabulary like "yesterday" and "tomorrow," but sometimes they confuse these words. "You missed the field trip tomorrow."

They understand daily time concepts like morning, afternoon and night, earlier, later, soon because they have heard these so often. It will be a long time, however, before they will be able to make sense of the clock on the wall.

Traditional "calendar activities" are generally a waste of time. Instead, talk about what you did yesterday, and what you will do today and tomorrow. Threes do not understand ordinal numbers (sixteenth, third, twenty-seventh). They may learn the name of the month, but it doesn't mean a lot to them yet.

MUSIC

Music, so basic to the human experience, gives children practice with language sounds, rhythm, and pitch. It is one very legitimate cultural activity you can do, exposing children to songs and music of different cultures. It is always a good social activity, something people do together.

Singing

Three-year-olds are at the point where they can really enjoy singing and other simple music activities. Threes can begin to carry simple tunes. Singing along with a group and remembering words to songs are useful exercises in becoming verbally expressive and help give children a feeling of belonging to the group as well. Most important, they are learning to enjoy the social aspects of music.

When teaching a new song, sing it slowly all the way through first so they can hear the whole thing. Then sing one line at a time and let them echo you. Then sing two lines at a time for them to echo. Repetition is the key. Don't just teach a new song for a week and then drop it. Sing all of their "learned" songs frequently. While "circle time" is one setting where children enjoy singing together, don't limit yourself to this time. Sing while you are outside, swinging on the swing, waiting for lunch, and any other free moment of the day. Music becomes a joyous expression. Don't be surprised if you hear children singing while they play with blocks, paint at the easel, or at other times during play.

Musical Circle Games and Creative Movement

Musical circle games like "Farmer in the Dell" are loved by three-year-olds and are good social activities. One good source book is *Wee Sing and Play,* by Pamela Conn Beall and Susan Hagen Nipp (Price/Stern/Sloan Publishers).

Free-form dancing and just plain moving to recorded music is also great fun for children, and allows them to express themselves with their whole body and learn to respond to the moods of music. They will enjoy waving such things as scarves, crepe paper streamers or pom poms to the music as well.

Simplified Musical Chairs

Simply arrange as many chairs as there are children facing alternately frontwards and backwards, the usual way for "Musical Chairs." Play recorded music and have children march around the chairs. When the music stops, they find a chair to sit in. DO NOT REMOVE A CHAIR, AS IS USUALLY DONE. Let the children repeat the sequence of marching around the chairs and sitting down when the music stops as often as their attention lasts. To add variety, you can challenge them to move in different ways as they go around the chairs: marching, tip-toeing, jumping, galloping, etc.

(The regular version of "Musical Chairs" in which one chair is removed each time and one child, left standing, is eliminated from the game is very distressing for three-year-olds, and therefore not recommended for this age.)

Rhythm Instruments

Rhythm instruments are fun for this age. Make them an available choice to play with during your free play time, so that children can explore them on their own. As a group activity, the most important thing you can do is have children learn some signal for when they are to stop playing – such as when you raise your hand up high. Practice starting and stopping over and over again. Then have children play the instruments in different ways such as soft and loud, fast and slow. Later, they can play along to recorded music. In the process they are learning about what makes different kinds of sounds, and are feeling elements of music.

Songs for Routines of the Day

Make up songs for the various times of your day, such as cleaning up, coming to the table, getting ready to go outside, or gathering at your circle time area. Fit your words to familiar melodies, such as "Twinkle, Twinkle Little Star," or "Farmer in the Dell." Acting according to the cues of simple songs is much more fun than responding to the commands of an adult.

HOW THEY PLAY

Their new social leanings dominate their play. Three-year-olds not only enjoy being near other children in parallel play situations, they begin to interact with other children in "cooperative play." There is still a great deal of imitative behavior in their play. One child will start doing something and everyone else wants to do that too. You may find lots of silliness and "behavior contagion," such as shrieking or running around together. They are just enjoying the pure joy of being together and having friends. Gradually they think of more interesting things to do.

Dramatic Play

The big new happening is their increased ability and enjoyment of dramatic play – "pretending" and putting themselves in a role, and "socio-dramatic play" – interacting with others from within their own roles. Again, their growing language capabilities make this possible. The child knows the difference between pretending and reality and gives certain signals to let others know she is pretending, such as a change in her voice, exaggerated facial expressions or a certain swagger in walk.

While many adults consider dramatic play "cute" but generally a waste of time, the opposite is true. This type of play has many benefits directly and indirectly related to academic learning. The psychological benefits are the best known. Children put themselves in roles of power when they pretend, taking control of scary situations. They are the doctor giving the shot or the powerful parent tucking the baby into bed. Their talk and gestures are often a parody of adults in their lives. Children's language is more complex when they interact with each other in dramatic play situations with more descriptive words. When they use objects and props for pretend, they are creating symbols for things they picture in their imagination. This relates to the ability to use symbols such as letters and numbers later on. Children who have spent a lot of time in dramatic play, literally putting themselves in someone else's shoes, seem to become more empathetic in real life, imagining how someone else feels.

The housekeeping corner is a very popular area of a preschool classroom and more informally at home. It is in this area particularly that children enjoy social contact with each other and can practice the "give and take" of natural social situations. Threes play out scenes in settings that are familiar to them and they are very familiar with what goes on in houses. Give it some extra space and "jazz it up" with interesting materials. Can you figure out a way to make several "rooms," rather than just having a kitchen? It would be fun to have a bedroom and a living room. Provide all kinds of props to add interest and variety to the play. Such things as placemats, throw rugs, bedding for a doll bed, lunch boxes, a block painted to look like a cellular phone, and of course, dress-up clothes and a mirror will add depth and variety to their play. Include "literacy" materials for them to weave into their play such as pencils, pens, note pads, shopping lists, magazines and newspapers, books, and an old computer keyboard.

As time goes on, think of other very familiar settings to create, such as a restaurant or grocery store. Instead of coming up with all the props yourself, invite the child or children to help you think of what you need. Perhaps take a trip to a neighborhood store and look around. Make a list with the children of what you see. Later, ask, "What could we use for..." You are helping the children to use their imaginations and come up with their own play ideas and props in the future.

In their actual play, the children may start out all doing pretty much the same thing. Two "mommies" might be feeding two "babies." This is still parallel play. Gradually, they will learn to elaborate and differentiate their roles. This can happen more easily if an adult occasionally plays along, taking on a minor role, such as a "neighbor," and helping children define different roles for themselves. Be careful to follow their lead and not to dominate their play. An experienced older child can also provide this benefit. Don't be too alarmed when you witness gender stereotyping in their play. They can be quite rigid in what they feel a "mommy" or "daddy" can do. Rather than being "preachy," just let them discover on their own, and through natural exposure to real people as well as books, the various roles available to men and women in our society.

Miniature Play

Playing with small people, animals and vehicles is extremely popular with this age and has many of the same benefits as dramatic play described above. The child becomes very powerful as she turns herself into a giant manipulating small figures, speaking for them and determining their fate. While there are many play settings manufactured for children of this age, which they do enjoy, also give them other materials they can use to create settings themselves, such as shoeboxes, other interesting small containers such as small plastic crates, pieces of cardboard, fabric, gift wrap tubing, etc. Much creative play with miniatures will happen in the block corner as well as with sand and water.

Blocks

Wooden unit blocks also provide potential for much social interaction, as well as quality solitary play where the child concentrates on how to use the material. When children are first exposed to blocks they may spend much time just lining them up to make "highways" or placing them side by side. They will pick up ideas from other children as well as from their own discovery process. The child will likely explore problems of balance and what shape will support other blocks. At first there may be a fascination with how tall a structure it is possible to make before it topples over.

Add cars, trucks, small animals and people, and the full range of imaginative play will open up. The highest level of block play is when they make structures and then use them in dramatic play, with miniature vehicles, animals and people, creating scenarios for their imagination. Is it any wonder blocks are so popular with three- and four-year-olds?

Creative Play

Three-year-olds enjoy all types of art experiences and materials, but they don't sit down to "create something," as an older child might. Instead, they simply enjoy experimenting with the material figuring out what they can make it do. If you watch a three-year-old paint, she will watch with interest as the color drips down the paper and discover with delight that she can spread it around. Often three-year-olds like to cover the whole paper with paint. Don't be surprised if layer after layer gets applied.

When they use crayons they explore in similar manner. You're likely to see round and round scribbles using many different colors.

Eventually their round shapes will connect to make a circle. It's common for the child to make "rays" coming out from the circle, like a sun or spider. A couple of dots for eyes might appear inside the circle and the number of "rays" begin to resemble arms and legs, still coming straight out of the circle, no body. Do not expect young children to color within lines or fill in spaces.

Scissors are fascinating. The child is just gaining the fine-motor skill to manipulate them and cut snips around the edge of the paper. (See the "fine motor" section above.) Add paste or glue and further experimentation will occur.

There are many good "how to" books on art activities for preschoolers which give you recipes and procedures. Keep art activities open-ended. You should not tell three-year-olds what to draw or paint or make. Give them the materials and show them how to use them correctly and then let them enjoy themselves, without having to live up to some product or idea assigned by an adult.

Sensory play materials such as sand, water, rice, mud, clay and play dough, will be enjoyed in the same way, rarely used to "make something" but just manipulated, poured, pounded and molded as the child discovers what she can do with the material.

Be sure to roll up children's sleeves and protect their clothing with waterproof smocks so they can relax and not worry about getting messy.

The Play Environment

The basic and traditional "interest centers" of a preschool classroom will be well-used by three-year-olds. These include:

- The housekeeping (dramatic play) corner, which should get the most space because it is their dominant interest
- An art and sensory play area
- A corner for blocks and accessories
- An area for constructive play with fine-motor materials
- A cozy book corner
- Places to enjoy musical instruments and "science" materials

These different areas should be well-defined and if possible, separated with furniture or dividers. This helps the child organize her environment in her mind, and makes it immensely easier for the adult to keep track of materials. While children may occasionally bring a toy or material from one area into another, it will be easier to clean up at the end of the play period. Let the children have a say in what to put where and label boxes and spaces on the shelf with photos or pictures to make them easier to find and put away again.

While the organization is likely to be less formal in a home setting, the wise parent can follow these same principles. Many parents have related how, after spending time in a well-organized preschool environment, their child came home and organized her bedroom or playroom into "interest centers."

Going Outside

Three-year-olds need time to run, climb, swing, slide and generally use their energy in a safe outdoor environment. Be sure to provide opportunities for dramatic play outside. Bring "props" outside, such as hats, capes, pretend binoculars, pieces of garden hose, and dishes and pots and pans to use in the sand area. They will need a hard surface to ride tricycles on. Sand, water, and messy art are often done most easily outside.

SUMMARY

Cooperative Play. Three-year-olds' new skills at interacting with other children deserve special attention. Your dramatic play area could easily be the focal point of your whole room. Set up many activities that are fun to do in the company of others.

Language. Blooming language abilities can be nourished through books, games, songs, science and art activities.

Moving. Activities that involve moving their bodies in different ways are fun and yet another way to be expressive while developing coordination.

CHAPTER 6

The Four-Year-Old

EXUBERANCE. That's the best single word to describe four-year-olds. Four-year-olds are enthusiastic, adventurous, bold, "out of bounds," silly, eager, fun. This is the pre-kindergarten year when there is a growing interest in letters and numbers and things academic, but they are not ready to "sit down and behave" for long periods of time. Life is too exciting.

Their interests center around such things as monsters, dinosaurs, and superheroes. Fours are very imaginative and they often express frightening themes in their imaginative play. They also like making faces, singing silly songs and being funny.

SOCIAL EMOTIONAL DEVELOPMENT

Issues of Emotional Development and Self-esteem

The phrase "out of bounds" also describes four-year-olds' emotions. They are expansive, bossy, boasting, and extreme in their emotions. They love things and hate things with intensity. With some sensitive guidance from adults, the child can begin to understand and name their emotions and then can learn acceptable ways to express them. It is a time when children are discovering their own personal power.

It's important that children learn about their emotions – that there are many ways people feel when things happen to them. They should learn how to identify what they are feeling. And most important, they should learn that there are no "bad"emotions. Everyone has a right to be angry, sad, afraid, happy, worried, etc. Then the major task (life-long, really) is learning acceptable ways of expressing those emotions.

Fears

As the child becomes part of the wider world with more experiences, he also becomes more vulnerable, sensing how little power he really has. Combine this with the preschooler's unspoken notion that thinking bad thoughts can make bad things happen, the child may be hauling around some guilt with him. The fears may show up as monsters in the closet or fear of dark places of the basement.

It's a time when many children have bad dreams from time to time. A sympathetic parent might suggest to the child that he "rewrite" his dream and make a better ending. "Dreams aren't real, although they feel that way. How would you like the dream to go?" The parent could help the child imagine vanquishing the monster that was chasing him, giving him a sense of personal power. It might also help to suggest pleasant things to dream about before the child goes to sleep. Give him the sense that he is the author of his dreams and has some control over them.

There are many fine picture books that focus on children's worries and fears. A children's librarian or a good children's book store could help you find titles. Books have the advantage of being neutral, not personal, so the child could get the sense that other children have also had thoughts like that, and were able to manage them.

Another thing that can make children fearful or anxious is facing new or scary situations, such as going to the doctor or the hospital, starting a new school situation, or even going to a birthday party. The best way to help the child is to rehearse what will happen. Visit the place ahead of time if possible. Show pictures. Let the child act out what will happen, using dolls or stuffed animals. Being able to anticipate what will happen makes everything feel more manageable.

A game four-year-olds can play is the "What would you do if..." game. Either one-on-one, in a small group, or with a puppet, you or the child could pose situations that might be frightening and talk about what the child might do. "What would you do if you were lost in the supermarket...afraid of the dark...go to a new school and don't know anybody...see a big dog down the street...?" When children figure out that there is usually something they can do to face a fear, it helps them to cope.

It is very common when a child has experienced something traumatic or fearful to replay it over and over again in his dramatic play. Whereas adults talk about something over and over again when they have been frightened, children play it over and over again, gradually coming to terms with it. Watching a child's play themes can sometimes give you insight into what is going on emotionally, but be careful not to over-interpret.

Relationships with Other Children

There is relatively little solitary play compared to earlier years. Of course, children will play by themselves from time to time, especially if they want to explore a new toy. However, they usually prefer to play with other children.

Friendships

You see four-year-olds developing strong friendships as they learn to play together in cooperative and creative ways. They define friendship in a very simple way – a friend is someone you play with. If they don't "play nice" with you, they're not your friend anymore. They often use the promise of friendship to manipulate each other. "If you don't give me that, I won't invite you to my birthday party." "I'll be your friend if you let me have a turn." They very much want to have someone to play with. This forces them to eventually consider the point of view of the other and do such difficult things as share and take turns.

Jealousy and Excluding

Four-year-olds have intense feelings, and jealousies often develop. Sometimes they have an all-or-nothing way of thinking as they develop "special" friends. "If you're my friend, you can't be her friend too." You might see children excluding other children from play, in an attempt to maintain their special status with their friend. This situation calls for sensitive intervention from the adult. Often bringing in one or two more children to the play group will help. Caution: groups of three can be difficult.

If you hear children excluding others on the basis of anything to do with their identity, such as skin color, gender or nationality, it is important to intervene and treat this the way you would other forms of aggression. As you talk to children, help build their ability to empathize by pointing out how the other person feels. Find ways of appreciating the uniqueness of every child yourself and it will help rub off on the other children. *The Anti-Bias Curriculum* by Louise Derman-Sparks and the A.B.C. Task force (NAEYC) gives you many valuable starting points.

There are many wonderful children's picture books about friendships which can help you get children talking about it. You could also have discussions, games, and pretend play about things to do to make someone feel good or be happy. You are teaching them friendship skills.

Sharing

Sharing materials and taking turns with toys are becoming a bit easier for four-year-olds, especially if they have had experience playing with other children under the sensitive supervision of an adult who can help them learn to negotiate and see the other child's point of view. They are less apt to protect possessions,

The adult can help the children learn to ask politely for a turn. They have enough command of language now to use words supplied to them and to remember them for future situations. Enlist their help in problem solving. "You both want this truck. How can we solve this problem?"

It should also be emphasized that if a child is in possession of a toy and another child asks for it, even politely, it is not absolutely necessary that the child turn over the toy immediately. He can learn polite responses, such as "I'm still using this, but I'll let you know when I'm done." If a child is expected to turn something over as soon as someone asks for it, it will be a long time before children see the benefit of taking turns. They have to feel their own rights of possession. If you feel a child is hanging on to something much too long, you could help him sense how the other child is feeling. "Martin has been waiting a long, long time for the car. He hopes you're almost done."

Give children plenty of positive practice. Plan activities that are more fun to do with someone else than alone, and which encourage children to share ideas. Dramatic play is ideal for this. Building something together with blocks, playing ball, and many other activities also encourage successful social interactions and strengthen feelings of friendship.

Typical Behavior Issues

Being exuberant and wild, four-year-olds need and feel safer and more secure with limits. Adults must state clearly what is and is not acceptable. If these limits are reasonable and remain consistent, children usually accept them well.

We know that adult models have a strong influence on how children handle frustration. If an adult's typical response is to lash out and hit the child or yell or call names, that is exactly what the child will do. The best route is to stop the child calmly and explain the reasons for not doing the offending action. Adults should always work on helping the child understand and care about how the other person is feeling. This builds the child's capacity for empathy.

It's interesting to know that preschool children may feel guilty after they do something they know is wrong, though they may not have enough self-control to stop themselves before they act. We need to help children develop a sense of personal responsibility for their behaviors. Not easy! One way is to involve them in problem solving. "What can we do to help you remember to ask instead of grabbing? You must be tired of hearing me tell you to stop all the time."

Aggression

After the age of three years old, boys and girls show a different pattern of aggression. Boys tend to become more and more physical, resorting to brawn, while girls learn to punish with words.

When physical aggression does occur, when one child hits, kicks, or otherwise hurts another child, this must not be ignored. The teacher must deal with it quickly and clearly. If an adult ignores aggression, children will think that the adult approves of the aggression. Even other children in the room not involved in the incident will come to this conclusion.

Four-year-olds, who are learning but certainly have not mastered inner controls of behavior, often want to lash out at their playmates, hurting them one way or another to get their way or make their point. It comes from the intensity of their feelings. The "bottom line" rule must always be, "No hurting people." A second rule can be, "No breaking things."

Again, we must make the child know that his feeling is legitimate, but not his actions. "I know you are angry, but it's not okay to hurt Angela. Let's figure out what else you could do to let her know how you feel." Then help him figure out how to do something constructive with his anger. Do not give double messages – your face and voice should match the message. Be stern without yelling.

Many teachers are distressed at children's worship of superheroes, and the aggression that it can lead to. It is true that television exposes children to a lot of violence, even in so-called "children's programs." Parents should be encouraged to limit the amount and type of television shows their children watch, and whenever possible, to watch the show with the children so they can help interpret what is going on.

It is interesting to know that part of the interest in violence seems to be developmental. Even if there were no TV, four-year-olds would still have violence in their imagination and their stories. It has to do with the issue of power. A child this age still feels quite vulnerable and has some fears. If he can identify with a superhero, it might feel easier to the child to conquer those fears.

Some teachers deal with the superhero issue by emphasizing the positive side of the heroes – how they help people and stand for "Truth, Justice and The American Way." It seems almost impossible to stop superhero play, so a better tactic may be to "manage" it. Allow superhero play only outside, and in a certain area of the playground, for instance. And children should not have to engage in this play unless they want to – in other words, no unwilling "victims."

Bullying

Bullying is not quite the same thing as aggression, although it may involve aggression. It is more of a "pecking order" issue. A child, often one with shaky self-esteem, wants to assert or maintain his personal power and so "lords it over" another child. They tend to pick on quiet, unassertive children.

The victim needs help – but not by you intervening and taking over the situation. Instead, teach the victim to use words to stick up for himself. If you can get a child to say forcefully, "That makes me mad!", or "I'm using this now. You can have it when I'm done," or "Stop! I don't like it when you kick me," instead of crying, running away or striking back, you are making progress. When the victim is able to assert himself, he seems less vulnerable and will be less likely to be picked on; in other words, not such an easy target.

All children need to learn how to express their own needs and feelings, and defend their own rights while respecting the rights and feelings of other children. If a child constantly cries and runs to an adult for help, that is rewarding the aggressor.

Still, a child does have a right to feel safe in the play environment. You have a responsibility to curtail aggressive acts.

Teasing

Teasing, taunting, name calling, and other types of insults are common with four-year-olds. Children are, indeed, learning to "use their words" but not always in the way we intend when we give that instruction. Teasing of this type, meant to hurt the feelings of someone else, is another form of aggression. It is a different way of hurting someone and can fall under your rule of "No hurting people."

This type of verbal aggression needs immediate and direct intervention from the parent, teacher or other caring adult. Point out calmly that words can definitely hurt people inside – "in their feelings" – and it's not okay to do that. Then don't just leave the child feeling ashamed or angry. Instead, acknowledge the frustration the child was feeling – whatever the situation was – and tell the child he has a right to express what he was feeling inside. Help him find the words. "I am making something using the big ball of clay and don't want to share it right now."

Inappropriate Language

Experimenting with swear words and "bathroom words" is also enormously interesting to four-year-olds. Again, he is experimenting with personal power. He has discovered that certain combinations of syllables "get a rise"out of people.

In many situations, the more an adult disapproves, the stronger the behavior will become. It might be best to ignore the outburst and either pretend you didn't hear it, or that it didn't affect you. However, that will not always work. Other children may still react and reinforce the behavior.

You can "disarm" the word by saying something like, "I heard the word, _____ over here...what's going on?" But do remember that you have rights, too. If a child's language genuinely offends you, you can say, "I don't like to hear that word here." Perhaps offer the child some other silly word to use instead. Or you may just give the matter of fact statement, "We don't want you to use those words here."

Try to distinguish when the outburst reflects genuine frustration, such as when a child drops his lunch or stubs his toe. That is not the time to talk about "nice words." Simply help him deal with the situation.

You might try launching into an intellectual discussion. "Isn't it interesting that certain sounds make people so upset?" One way to negate the impact of swear words in the classroom is to make up your own silly swear words. Then pretend to be offended and shocked when they say them. "Did you hear that!!! He called me a snickelnose!!!"

Lying

It is not uncommon for four-year-olds to stretch the truth, or come out with real "whoppers." It does not mean they are destined for a life of treachery. For one thing, there is still enough "magic" left in their world that sometimes wishing for something hard enough actually makes them believe the fantasy is true. Some of the time the lying is in the form of denial. The child wishes strongly that he had not done something, or that an event had not taken place. It can be a form of "saving face." Most of the time, their lying is an attempt to redesign reality.

The best way to deal with it is with empathy. "I know you wish that teddy bear was yours, but it belongs to Jennifer."

No Apologies Necessary

It's best not to force four-year-olds to apologize. If an apology occurs spontaneously and is sincere, that's great. But usually, because a four-year-old is still very egocentric, the "I'm sorry," is merely a manipulative device to regain favor. If you force it, you may just be teaching children to be hypocritical.

A better way for a child to "make up" to another child is to help correct the situation – help rebuild the block tower he knocked down, clean up a mess, or put something back.

Re-establish a Relationship with the Child

As a general statement, whenever you have to impose limits on children, deal with their aggression or correct their behavior, be sure to give them another start with a clean slate. It is usually wise after a conflict to involve the child in something totally different. Often play with toys he can use by himself or play with sensory materials is calming and allows the child to pull himself together again. Also, try to re-establish a pleasant relationship with the child yourself. Settle down and play with the child, letting him know he hasn't "blown it" with you forever. If a child feels you don't like him any more, he won't be motivated to please you with good behavior and his self-esteem will suffer, strengthening negative behaviors.

GROSS MOTOR DEVELOPMENT

Four-year-olds are expansive in their movements. They run fast, climb high, gallop, jump and hop. There seems to be energy and "push" behind everything they do. They like to spin around to make themselves dizzy, or hook their hand around a pole and twirl around it. A very "physical" age! A wise teacher will build an active physical component into most activities. Remember that young children need to move and be active in order to understand concepts.

This is the age when people are most likely to label a child "hyperactive." Often, upon closer examination, it will turn out that the child is simply exhibiting the high energy typical of the age and is not provided with enough outlet for this energy. It's when adults expect four-year-olds to sit still for too long that trouble brews.

It's important to think about how to handle this high energy load. One solution is to provide ample outdoor time, when they can engage their loud voices as well as their muscles for running and climbing. A playground or yard with a good climber and space to run and ride tricycles is invaluable. Circle games, follow-the-leader games, "chases," monster play, are all fun outside.

The main trick is to determine how much out-of-bounds behavior you can allow, and when to "put the lid on." Don't make everyone miserable by expecting four-year-olds to sit still for long periods of time. Build in plenty of relaxed play time when children can play at their own energy level. It may help to have a very vigorous activity just before you want them to settle down for awhile, to "get the wiggles out." Relax and enjoy it when you can. Take part in the silliness.

Four-year-olds enjoy any activity that allows them to use their muscles. Creative movement and dancing are great fun (see the music section below). They enjoy all kinds of circle games, as long as they don't have to wait, doing nothing until it is their turn. Activities involving hula hoops, balls, beanbags, parachutes and ropes will all attract much interest and eager participation.

<u>*Can You Do What I Do?*</u>

One favorite follow-the-leader circle game is to chant:

"Can you do what I do, I do, I do....
Can you do what I do, just like me?"

A "leader" then demonstrates any kind of motion, and the others imitate it. It's fun to add a sound with the motion. Then go to the next person in the circle to be the leader and demonstrate a different motion to copy. Go all the way around the circle. Younger fours may choose the same motion the first leader chose. You might decide that's okay, as long as they're having fun.

Bad Weather Survival

Nobody watches weather forecasts with greater interest than a teacher of four-year-olds. Bad weather survival is an important skill of people who work with this age group. Think of active indoor games children can enjoy, and keep them special for the time of day when you would ordinarily have been outside. The balloon tennis game described in the chapter on two-year-olds, page 75, will still be greatly enjoyed by four-year-olds. Dancing while waving around long crepe paper streamers will also use up energy. Having target practice with the "soft balls" made from pantyhose and polyester fiberfill stuffing is fun indoors. (See page 55.)

Add other things to your "Rainy Day Kit" like special board games, dress-up clothes, flashlights and art materials that may only be brought out when it rains and they can't go outside. Who knows? You and the children might even look forward to rainy days! (Nah!)

Need for Rest

It is often at the age of four-and-a-half or slightly later that some children have real trouble settling down and falling asleep at nap time. And yet, if they do not rest well in the middle of the day, the afternoons can be rough. There are some four-year-olds who simply cannot fall asleep, yet the high energy demands of this age really need to be met by a period of rest. Non-sleepers should not be forced to lie quietly on a cot or mat for the entire nap period while other children are sleeping. This is as close to torture as you can get for a high-energy four-year-old, and could make him hate coming to your program. After a reasonable time of his lying quietly and trying to sleep – a half-hour, say – give him an alternative. Allow him to get up and engage in some quiet activities such as looking at books, listening to story tapes using headphones, or playing with snap-together blocks (in another room if possible).

It will be to your advantage to calm children down as much as possible before nap time. It can start before lunch. Gather the group together after an active morning with a short group discussion that recaps the morning and looks forward to the afternoon. A good story fits in nicely here. Lunch should be pleasant and unrushed. Start talking in a quieter voice. Anticipate nap time pleasantly. "Ah, soon we'll be able to stretch out on our cots and close our eyes and relax." Yawn a lot. When everyone is lying down is another ideal time for a story, especially if you tell the story rather than read a book. Tell them to see the pictures in their imagination. Take care not to make the story too exciting or you'll have them all revved up again! Deep breathing, soft music, lullabies, and back rubs help too. (Sounds great, doesn't it?)

FINE MOTOR DEVELOPMENT

Fours are getting skillful at using their hand muscles. They can button, zip, lace shoes (but usually not tie shoes), string small beads, cut with scissors, pour juice. While they will enjoy printing the letters of their names, the letters will be large and awkward. It is not the time to sit children down for a writing lesson.

There is a wide variety of toys manufactured to allow children to use their developing fine-motor skills. These include small wooden cubes to build with, beads to string, wooden inlay puzzles and simple jigsaw puzzles, construction toys with many fit-together pieces, and pegs and pegboards. Remember also that the art activities you offer children all offer fine-motor practice.

Lacing Cards

Make your own simple lacing cards. Glue a simple picture from a magazine onto thin cardboard and laminate it or use clear contact paper on the front and back. Use a single-hole punch to punch holes around the outline of the picture. Cut pieces of yarn for the children to "sew" through the holes and stiffen the ends of the yarn with tape.

Self-help Skills

Like three-year-olds, but more so, four-year-olds really love to be helpful in daily routines, and enjoy feeling important and useful.

If you put juice and milk in small pitchers, children have reasonable success pouring their own drinks. (Provide valuable practice in your water play activities.) Have a sponge handy and show children how to clean up their own spills.

They do just fine feeding themselves. Model good manners, but do not harp on them. Exuberant and silly four-year-olds often pick mealtime to imitate each other, make faces and play with their food. Certainly, it is appropriate for the adult to put a limit on this. That is one good reason teachers should sit down at the table and eat with four-year-olds, more or less guiding the discussion in a different direction when it starts to get out of hand.

Almost all four-year-olds have mastered the entire routine of going to the bathroom. You will probably have to give frequent reminders about handwashing.

But that is not the major problem. Four-year-olds need supervision in the bathroom because they are very interested in bathrooms in general, and other children in particular. Silliness and "bathroom talk" is very typical. It is the prime age for "you show me yours, and I'll show you mine." Although this curiosity is natural, the child care setting is not the appropriate place for gaining information. If you do happen upon children engaged in exploratory behaviors, put a stop to it in a matter of fact manner.

A Grooming Center

Set up a mirror in your room and have a comb or brush for each child, with his name on it. These could be stored in separate compartments of a hanging shoe bag. Encourage children to wash their faces and then comb their own hair after getting up from nap or coming in from outside.

LANGUAGE DEVELOPMENT

The silliness and expansiveness of a typical four-year-old's personality, of course, carry over to language. Most four-year-olds have become quite facile with language, and now they can afford to fool around with it. They enjoy playing with words and making up new, funny words and sounds. They love exaggerations and words like "enormous," "gigantic," "colossal." They enjoy extremes in their voices, shouting, whispering, and telling "secrets." Four is a noisy age; they are loud in almost everything they do. Teachers of fours are often heard admonishing, "Use your indoor voice."

Four-year-olds have a lot to say. It used to be that they mainly labeled objects or actions in front of them. Now they can talk about things they can't see at the moment – ideas, "what if's." You'll also hear four-year-olds chattering away for the pure pleasure of it, making up silly words, chanting nonsense rhymes and making up what they consider "jokes."

In a group setting, most of their language is now directed at other children rather than adults, although they are good at asking adults for help. They can sustain play with other children for as long as twenty or thirty minutes with good reciprocal conversation throughout. They like to give information, and greatly enjoy some one-on-one talking time with favorite adults.

Some four-year-olds go through a period of stuttering. Their ideas get so big that their mouth cannot keep up. Don't correct the child or try to finish his words or sentences for him. Just wait patiently for him to get it out.

This is also known as the age of "Why?" Sometimes the "Why's" are a genuine quest for information about the infinite mysteries of the universe, and sometimes they are simply a ploy to extend the attention of the adult. If you make a thoughtful attempt to answer the incessant questions you are likely to encourage an inquiring mind. Don't hesitate to say, "I don't know." Also ask, "What do you think?" "Let's find out," is another wonderful response.

Story Telling

Four-year-olds now have enough language comprehension that they can enjoy a story that is told without a picture book, rather than read to them. To follow the story they have to rely only on the spoken words, without any visual clues.

You might start out with easy stories about the children themselves in familiar surroundings: "Once upon a time there was a class of children, and they had the most wonderful teacher in the world. First thing in the morning two fine boys came in the room. Their names were Caleb and Scott. Scott said, 'Let's feed the rabbit...'" and you go ahead and relate the events of the morning in your own room They will listen with rapt attention, filling in some of the details as you go.

Later you can go on to more traditional stories like "Little Red Riding Hood" or your own made-up fairy tales.

Child Dictated Stories

Invite a child to tell you a story. A child is often so pleased at the undivided attention of an adult that he will eagerly comply. To extend the child's use of language, you might offer some questions: "Then what happened?" "Was she afraid?" "Did anyone come along?" Tape recording these stories adds importance to them and children will enjoy listening to them again and again.

Art work is often accompanied by spontaneous stories or explanations. Grab a pencil and write the words down as the child dictates, but hang onto your hat and don't be surprised at the violence that emerges – "...and then the monster came along and bashed his head in." That's typical of four-year-olds. Write his story down without judgmental statements. The child is learning about the power of words.

Picture Matching Games

Picture matching games give good opportunities for vocabulary development and comprehension. Buy two copies of the same magazine and cut the same pictures out of each. Glue one set of pictures to a large card. Glue the matching pictures to small cards. Have several different sets of these, with different pictures. Give each child a large card, and you keep the small cards, mixed up. You can play this at several different levels:

- *Simple matching. You are working on the concept of "same and different" here. You show the child a small card and say, "Is there a picture on your card that is the same as this?" You can help the child make the judgment by holding the small card next to the pictures on the card and comparing details.*

• Show a card to the children and ask, "What's this?" Have the child produce the word. "That's right, this is a wagon. Do you have a wagon on your card?"

• Describe what is on the small card without showing it to the children. "This is a piece of fruit that grows on a tree. It is red. When you bite it, it crunches. Sometimes we drink juice made from this fruit." Children must understand your words and get a visual image in order to make a match.

Puppets

Four-year-olds, with their capable imaginations and growing abilities to produce language, have fun with puppets. They will not put together elaborate plays or even dialogues with other puppets, although there may be some play between puppets. Homemade puppets are just as good (and often better than) purchased puppets. You don't need a puppet stage, although children will enjoy using a large box turned into a theater.

Puppets allow children to take on silly voices, to roar, to pretend to bite, to sing silly songs. In other words, puppets allow children an outlet for many of the things that are typical of being four-year-olds, which may not always be considered socially acceptable for real people to do.

If a teacher has a "pet puppet," or two, with special personalities and voices, children will be even more resourceful in their use of puppets the teacher makes available to them.

Group Discussions

Four-year-olds have the attention span for brief group discussions, especially if they are interesting. "What would you do if..." discussions can be successful with four-year-olds. "What would you do if you got lost in the supermarket?" Use this idea also for fun with imaginations. "What would you do if you found a talking toad on the playground?" "What would you do if you suddenly discovered you could fly?" Sometimes the books you read to the children can be the starting point for discussions.

In your discussions with children, try to keep a good portion of your questions "open-ended." Don't ask questions that have one right answer, or a "yes" or "no" answer. Example of a closed question: "What was the dog's name?" (The answer will either be the right name or a wrong name, or an "I don't know.") Example of an open question: "What would you do if a dirty dog like Harry ran into the house?" (Any answer is acceptable.)

Show and Tell

Show and tell, the old nursery school classic where one child at a time stands up and shows some object brought from home and talks about it, is designed to give children experiences in speaking in full sentences and sharing ideas in front of a group. Often this activity produces less than ideal results. Many times it seems to be a session of "bring and brag" instead of show and tell, as children try to outdo each other with their superhero toys. Sometimes a normally exuberant child might stand up in front of friends he plays with every day and stare at his feet, unable to utter a word. (This is too young to have to suffer the agonies of stage fright!) Then there are always the children who want to dominate and go on and on, while other children find it very hard to wait their turn.

There are some good variations. If it is more spontaneous it seems to work well. A child comes in with a box of new kittens. Now, that's something to talk about! If children are made to feel that they can tell the group about something interesting any time it is more natural. Some teachers limit show and tell to one day a week, and ask parents to help children find something that relates to the "unit" or "theme" they are working on. Try a "Nature Show and Tell." Children may bring in objects for the science table and talk about where they found it, what it is, etc.

Early Literacy

Still, the best way you can create eager readers later on is to provide a language-rich environment where children learn to use language purposefully and successfully. Include meaningful discussions in your day. Listening skills gained in group activities and enjoying books are a major part of being ready to learn to read. Tell stories, and encourage the children to do the same, as described above. Read to them with obvious pleasure. Provide lots of print materials in the environment – books, signs, magazines, labels for things that are important to them – and place writing materials in many places.

This pre-kindergarten child is becoming interested in naming letters and sometimes picking out words he knows. Don't force this on children in large doses, but if the interest is spontaneous, encourage it. Many four-year-olds will pretend to write letters and read books. The main "danger" with four-year-olds is that the teacher, sensing their abilities, will overdo it, and put too much focus on trying to teach children to read. It is very hard for energetic four-year-olds to sit quietly doing "seat work" for very long. Use active games and activities to teach concepts and stay tuned-in to their energy level and interest. Be careful not to turn learning to read into a negative experience.

Books

Whereas three-year-olds like nice, gentle books about families, animals and familiar things, four-year-olds like books that are adventurous or silly. Books about giants, monsters, dinosaurs, animals in people roles and machines have great appeal. Maurice Sendak's *Where the Wild Things Are* can be a bit too threatening and scary for three-year-olds. It is, however, the all-time favorite for four-year-olds. Poetry, especially funny poetry, will catch their interest.

Four-year-olds enjoy complexity in illustrations in their books. They like to search for a small object on a page and gaze at the beautiful colors and patterns of well done art work.

COGNITIVE DEVELOPMENT

In all his "Why?" questions the four-year-old is also showing a genuine curiosity. He wants to know how things work and the causes of what happens. This shows his increased capacity for thinking about ideas and things not immediately visible to him. However, four-year-olds still have a hard time dealing with abstract concepts, so stay away from explanations that go beyond what children can see and touch. But, do help them to see more. They are interested in what is real and what is not real. They want to know what's inside of things, like rocks. They want to see the back side of everything. They may get interested in what "dead" is when they see a dead animal on the road. Keep a piece of fruit or your Halloween pumpkin around (in a covered container) and let mold grow.

The four-year-old's brain is becoming more and more able to use symbols – pictures, signs, labels, sounds that represent something else. It's important to remember the "body connection." They have to move and handle materials. An active body with the sensory input that comes from touching, seeing, and hearing gives the brain more to "hang on to" as concepts are learned.

Imagination

At four, the imagination of children is flourishing. They love adventure, excitement, excursions, anything new. Children three and under have been pretty busy just figuring out how the world works, and the flexibility in their thinking has been limited. But by now, they have had enough experiences with the world to sense its infinite possibilities. Their imagination shows up in much of what they do.

Time Concepts

Four-year-olds are more and more able to understand designations of time. Although it's still not recommended to spend much time doing "calendar" activities, many four-year-olds can recite the days of the week and the seasons of the year. Understanding clock time is still beyond most children this age, but they will learn that certain things happen at certain times of the day. Lunch is at 11:30, or a favorite TV show comes on at 4:00. They may still mix up yesterday, today and tomorrow in their own speech, but understand it when adults use these terms.

The Senses Lead

Concepts useful in recognizing letters and words as well as mathematic concepts, such as shapes, size, volume and part/whole relationships, are learned through the senses. Puzzles, pouring sand, constructing with blocks and many other play activities, as well as adult-led activities like cooking, give children real life experiences with these concepts – the best way to learn at this age. Of course, there is no lack of counting books and shape books on the market, some of them rather well done, but these will serve best as reinforcers of what children have learned through their senses in play experiences.

Sorting

As children start to think about things and organize their universe, they notice various ways that things are alike and different. Sorting activities of all types reinforce this skill. Here are two:

<u>*Category Matching*</u>

Put different categories of pictures on each large card. For example, mammals on one, birds on another, fish on a third, and reptiles on a fourth. Children are therefore forming mental categories as they are matching cards. Other possible categories: tools, toys, cars, trucks, airplanes, boats, food, flowers, trees, etc.

<u>*Go Together Matching*</u>

The child must match up pictures on the large card and the small cards that are not the same, but go together such as a toothbrush and toothpaste, soap and a washcloth, car and car keys, horse and saddle, etc.

Sequencing

Sequencing involves remembering the order of events. As children do this, they learn such words as "before," "first," "next," and "last." These are all important concepts for reading and making sense out of a story. Cooking projects provide opportunities for learning because things must be done in a certain order. Here are some other fun ways to reinforce this skill:

<u>*Walk Sequence*</u>

Go on a walk with the children and bring along a camera. (An "instant" camera or a digital camera is best so the memory of the experience is fresh for the children.) Take a picture every few minutes, based on what you are doing or seeing. Later, when all the pictures are available, mix them all up and let the children help you arrange them in the order they happened.

<u>*Special Event Report*</u>

Something special happened and your puppet slept through the whole thing. Let a child tell the puppet what happened, "blow by blow." If the story gets confusing, or out of order, let the puppet ask clarifying questions.

Ordering

Lining things up from little to big is something four-year-olds like to do. Find all sorts of things they can do this with such as shoes, rocks, stuffed animals and people. Later they can organize things by such categories as light to dark, light to heavy, and smooth to rough.

MUSIC

Four-year-olds like to sing, and they especially enjoy silly songs. *Wee Sing Silly Songs* by Pamela Conn Beall and Susan Hagen Nipp (Price/Stern/Sloan Publishers), is a collection of many of the funny songs you remember from childhood.

The loud noises of rhythm instruments are also very appealing to fours. How about a rhythm band parade around the playground, flag and all? Dancing and moving to some of the excellent early childhood music on the market is also a popular activity with four-year-olds.

HOW THEY PLAY

Dramatic Play

The vivid imagination of four-year-olds feeds dramatic play of all types. You see it everywhere, in planned and unplanned situations.

The "house corner" with child sized furniture, dolls and dress-up clothes remains one of the favorite places in the preschool classroom, as it was when the child was three. But their play has become more elaborate. Where three-year-olds were fairly rigid in the family roles they played, four-year-olds can think of many more roles to play.

Four-year-olds will also greatly enjoy pretend play in different settings. Use furniture, boxes and props to create such settings as a restaurant, a television studio, a bus, an airplane, a rocket ship, the seashore, the post office, a beauty shop, a campsite, etc.

It is important to keep in mind that boys enjoy fantasy play just as much as girls. Dress-up clothes and props should accommodate the male roles as well as female roles. There are some boys who never seem to want to play in the house corner. Perhaps some subtle early social conditioning has already taken hold and they don't want to be caught playing with dolls. Where do they choose to play instead? Usually in the block corner where they become construction bosses, highway engineers, and giants – still very much in the realm of fantasy play! When play settings are varied as described above, we usually see eager participation from boys as well as girls. Boys engage in more dramatic play outdoors than indoors. They can range farther, run, shout, and act out the adventurous roles that appeal to them most.

You see dramatic play everywhere children play. A tricycle becomes a car, an ambulance, a fire engine. A climber turns into a rocket ship, a burning building, a cage in the zoo. A crayon becomes a race car zooming around the paper track.

What is the Value of Dramatic Play?

Most people are quite accepting of house play with three-year-olds. With an emphasis on "push your child," however, one hears more and more pressure to get the pre-kindergarten child to abandon fantasies and "get down to the business of learning." What a mistake this would be! Time spent pretending is time well-spent.

The social advantage of pretend play with other children, of course, continues. In the give and take without adult intervention or leadership, children sort out who they are and how to get along with others.

The word "imagination" shares a root with the word "image." If a child can imagine himself as big and capable, and act it out often, he is more likely to become big and capable. Through fantasy play, the child rehearses life experiences and roles.

A child with a rich experience in fantasy play develops flexibility in thinking, and is better able to cope with change and stress later in life. The outward dramatic play of the child becomes the daydreaming and private fantasies of the adult. One must first imagine oneself in a better situation before being able to take action for change. Children sometimes play out an unpleasant or frightening experience of real life. In the process they gain control of their fears.

When children create props for their play, they are creating and using their own symbols. They know the paper plate isn't a steering wheel. They have a mental image of a steering wheel and use the paper plate prop to represent it. They also learn to use gestures for symbols. This all makes it easier for children to use the symbols of letters and numbers to aid and anchor their thinking later on.

Imitating the exploits of superheroes may dominate the dramatic play of some children. Teachers are concerned because often the play is less complex and stems less from the child's own agenda than "regular" dramatic play. Often, it seems, children are simply imitating scenes they have seen on television and the characters have a very narrow range of possible behaviors.

Teachers or parents might play along as a secondary character occasionally to try to add depth to the characters, give them more feelings than are portrayed on TV, or suggest ways they could become helpers. While you might not prohibit this form of play, do try to give children suggestions for a wide range of roles different from superheroes as well.

Blocks

Wooden unit blocks and large hollow blocks are greatly enjoyed by four-year-olds. Combined with cars and trucks, plastic dinosaurs, plastic zoo or farm animals, and little people, children use blocks to create scenes for their imaginations.

A great deal of language skill is developed in the block corner. There is oral communication as children explain their structures and develop imaginative play around trains, airports, hotels, etc. The following activities are ways in which the teacher can structure block play to develop an understanding of shape, size, number, and similarities and differences.

<u>*Same Blocks, Different People*</u>

Give two children exactly the same number and shape of blocks. Tell them to make something with the blocks, but don't let them see each other as they build. When they are both finished have children see how similar or different their constructions are.

<u>*Exact Copies*</u>

Give two children exactly the same number and shape of blocks and challenge them to make buildings that are exactly the same. They will really have to work together closely and notice shapes and sizes!

The large hollow blocks can be made into something "huge" (a favorite word). Usually building something with large blocks is a cooperative effort with other children. They are great fun for stretching the imagination.

Creative Play

It is in this year that children usually begin drawing things which look like something recognizable. Three-year-olds mainly scribbled, or at most, made circles with faces in them. Four-year-olds will typically start "doodling," making random lines on the paper, and then suddenly notice that the lines resemble something. Then they will add details and tell you a wild story about it! Do refrain from telling children what to draw. Let the ideas come from them.

They will take great delight in the whole range of art projects. Give them many different materials to work with over time and let them explore the possibilities.

Sensory play with such materials as water, play dough, clay, sand and mud often spans dramatic and creative play. Add little people and animals or dishes and pots and pans as accessories. Wooden blocks added to the sand area can produce some very interesting and creative play.

Games

Games with rules, even simple board games designed for young children, are very difficult for four-year-olds – emotionally. They hate to lose! They will cheat, "fudge," demand another turn and be extremely upset if a co-player gets the best of them. Competition is painful. When four-year-olds have a race from one side of the yard to the other, each may declare himself the winner.

The Play Environment

Indoors, the typical "interest centers" of the preschool classroom – housekeeping/dramatic play; blocks; art; music; science; books; manipulatives, etc. – may look similar to the setup in a room designed for three-year-olds, but they contain different things – more complex toys, more varied props, things that will allow the child to use his imagination.

Organization is even more important because four-year-olds move fast and are impulsive. Knowing exactly where they can find something will allow them to be creative in their play. It also allows for quicker clean-up.

Going Outside

The outside environment takes on increasing importance in this year. Four-year-olds need space for their high energy. Climbing, running, riding tricycles and other riding toys, playing with gross-motor equipment are almost necessities for four-year-olds. The whole classroom and curriculum in a preschool setting could conceivably be brought outside in good weather.

SUMMARY

Imagination. This word says it all. In all of your activities, be they art, science, children's literature, movement, dramatic play or blocks, the imagination should dominate. If you can encourage and stretch the natural imagination and curiosity of four-year-olds, not squelch them, you are giving them a valuable gift and tool for later life. You will have created "eager learners," children who want to know more.

Learning to recognize letters and numbers, shapes, sizes and colors can be a secondary focus, preparing children for the kindergarten year ahead. All such "pre-academic" learning activities should be accomplished through active play and fun picture books, because fours are not ready for formal learning.

CHAPTER 7

The Five-Year-Old

WHEREAS THE FOUR-YEAR-OLD was wild and "out of bounds," the five-year-old is composed and "together." The typical five-year-old is calm, serene, wants to be good, and generally looks on the sunny side. The five-year-old loves to be read to, and talked to, and likes to learn new facts – ideal for kindergarten!

SOCIAL EMOTIONAL DEVELOPMENT

The five-year-old is generally a very pleasant person to be around. She likes to help, and loves praise. She has ideas and loves to talk about them. She can judge pretty well what she can and cannot do, and is fairly self-limiting.

Some children go through a difficult period at around five-and-a-half when they may become brash, disobedient, over-demanding and explosive. These children may also tend to dawdle, and be less coordinated than they were before. It usually doesn't last long if treated with patience and understanding.

Fives usually respond well to praise and empathetic listening. A short time apart from other children to pull themselves together again often helps when a child is having trouble controlling herself.

Issues of Emotional Development and Self-esteem

A five-year-old's sense of self-esteem comes from feeling capable. They like to do things "the right way." They take comfort in knowing the rules and specific expectations for behavior because it is easier to do something "right" and be "good." At this age they are quite inflexible in their thinking about right and wrong.

They are firmly convinced that good is rewarded and evil is punished, which explains some of the appeal of old, traditional folk tales. There is a dark side to this belief. When something bad happens in their life, they are often convinced it is their fault. "When I do something bad, I get punished. Something bad happened, therefore I must have done something wrong." It's important at times of crisis – divorce, sickness in the family, even a natural disaster – that adults take the time to reassure the child that she did nothing to cause the situation. It is not her fault.

Fives also take pride in what they can do with their body – climb high, run fast, do "tricks." They "show off" a lot and may also be boastful.

They adore teachers and other important adults in their lives. They really soak up positive attention and praise.

Relationships with Other Children

"The group" is becoming more and more important. Five-year-olds crave a feeling of friendship and acceptance from other children. The friendships of five-year-olds can be solid and enduring. Rather than being based merely on who is playing with you at the moment, a five-year-old's friendships are based on mutual interests.

By age five, children have a strong preference for playing with children of their own sex, and this will continue for several years. They haven't quite developed the "aversion" for the other sex that we see later in the middle years, however. Generally it's best to let the children choose their playmates, although if you see them excluding another child because of gender (or any other reason connected to the child's identity) you need to intervene.

Typical Behavior Issues

Whatever the conflict or behavior problem, use it as an opportunity to teach problem solving. "What could you do when this happens again?" It is important to acknowledge how frustrating it can be when things don't go as you planned. You are not telling a child that she must always give in to another child, but helping her learn effective and considerate ways to express herself that don't hurt feelings.

Quarreling and Excluding

It is an age of "squabbling." Sometimes they just seem to argue for the sake of arguing, almost as if they are practicing new verbal skills. If you feel that's the case, it might be best to simply divert the children to a new activity to give them a fresh start, or in some cases, different activities, separate from each other.

Whereas younger preschoolers usually fight over toys, conflicts among five-year-olds are more about social issues – who gets to play with whom, what roles each will play, whom they like, whom they don't like. This can be very painful. It can also be difficult for you to know how to intervene effectively. If one child is excluded or picked on by other children, it seems the more you stick up for that child, the worse it gets.

In some cases it seems arbitrary. They pick on another child for no apparent reason. At other times you'll be able to see what the excluded child is doing to turn the others off. It may be that she is overly bossy, always insisting on her own way. Or it could be that she doesn't blend in with the play theme of the others. In these cases there may be things you can do to coach the child in some play skills, figuring out how to create a role for herself that can build on what the players are already doing. Always work to strengthen the group's sense of empathy, pointing out the other child's point of view, and if possible, get the other child to describe how she feels.

Stealing

Taking things that belong to others and then lying about it is one of the more common behavior problems among five-year-olds. Because they want so much to be good, it is hard for them to admit when they have yielded to temptation.

"Accidents"

Sometimes fives have a hard time telling the difference between an accident and something another child does on purpose. For instance, one child might turn a somersault and by accident knock over a block structure. This may make the builder very angry and want to hit back. Naturally, you teach the one who caused the accident to say, "I'm sorry. It was an accident. I didn't mean to knock it over." Then that child could help rebuild the block tower. It seems, though, that some children catch on to this quickly and even with purposeful acts, immediately say, "It was an accident."

GROSS MOTOR DEVELOPMENT

In contrast to the expansive four-year-old, the five-year-old is poised and controlled. Arms are generally held close to the body. Skipping is a new skill for five-year-olds. All kinds of movement activities and dance usually appeal to this age group.

In playing with a ball, boys and girls have developed their characteristically different styles of throwing. Boys will throw a ball with a sideward stroke of the arm, and girls throw overhand. Depending on the amount of experience they have had, both boys and girls can be fairly successful at catching a medium sized ball.

Tricycles and other wheeled riding toys are still fun. There are some fine riding toys designed for cooperative play which have great appeal for five-year-olds.

They love to show off their physical skills doing "tricks," climbing, jumping from high places, etc.

FINE MOTOR DEVELOPMENT

By age five, it is usually evident whether the child is right-handed or left-handed. Do not try to force a left-handed child to use her right hand for writing and drawing. Have left-handed scissors available to avoid frustration for those children.

Writing

Fives are ready to begin printing letters on lined paper, although for some it is still very difficult.

A five-year-old can hold a pencil correctly when shown how and likes to make lines, letters, and drawings. Provide a variety of writing and drawing implements such as colored pencils, ball point pens, fine line felt-tipped markers and crayons.

Coloring

Five-year-olds are gaining skills at coloring within outlines. Rather than using coloring books, which may inhibit creativity, give the child cookie cutters, stencils or templates to trace around and then color within the lines. She will enjoy making various patterns and designs, and her creativity will be encouraged rather than stifled.

Manipulatives

Lacing cards, puzzles with many pieces, sewing with large yarn needles and burlap in hoops, making patterns with small colored pegs and peg boards, and fit-together bricks are all popular with five-year-olds, giving them practice with their eye-hand coordination, and making patterns.

Self-help Skills

Some, but not all, five-year-olds can tie their shoes. Most can button, and zip jackets with bottom opening zippers.

LANGUAGE DEVELOPMENT

The language skills of five-year-olds are well developed and they enjoy talking about a wide range of subjects. At home, parents could help the child think about what she wants to tell Dad at the end of the day, or something Grandmother would like to hear about.

News Board

Often children will arrive in the morning bursting to tell you something. "My grandfather came to our house for a visit! He came on a train!" Establish a "news" bulletin board for such items. Then you can say, "That sounds like something for our news board. Let's write it down." Let the child dictate the words to you. You might invite her to draw a picture to go with it. Then post it on the board. During your group time, have those children who have posted news items read them, or tell about them to the rest of the class. This process has allowed the child to "rehearse" her words, and is a pre-reading exercise.

I Spy

This familiar guessing game is fun to play with five-year-olds. "I see something in this room that's made of plastic and it's round, and you blow it up, and it has yellow, blue, red, and white sections and it bounces." Children must not only use their listening and comprehension skills but also their deductive thinking skills in eliminating possible answers one by one.

After children have a lot of experience playing this game with the adult as the one who chooses and describes the object, let them take on the challenge of being the person to describe the mystery object. That takes real skill in producing the right words, and deciding what to say about an object without naming it.

Fill-in-the-Blank Stories

Children are especially good at this if you have read many stories to them. You supply connecting phrases, and they fill in the colorful and exciting details. The point is not for the child to retell a familiar story, but to make up a new story. Any fill-in word that fits the context of the teacher's preceding phrase is acceptable. In the process, children not only exercise their imagination but get a valuable experience in listening, logical thinking and context of language. This is great fun to do with a small group.

Teacher:	*"Once upon a time there was a...*
Child:	*Bear!*
Teacher:	*This bear was very, very...*
Child:	*Big.*
Teacher:	*In fact, this bear was so big, he couldn't...*
Child:	*fit in his cave.*
Teacher:	*'Oh dear,' said the bear. 'What shall I do?' He sat down and started to..."*

These stories can be wonderful fun and allow the expansive imagination of a group of five-year-olds to really take off. It's fun to tape record these stories and later transcribe them into a book.

Poetry

Poetry gives a child the opportunity to play with words and enjoy the richness of the sounds. It's a lucky child who has a teacher or parent who can share the love of poetry. The surest way to kill an interest in poetry is to force children to memorize and recite it. On the other hand, if the adult shows obvious enjoyment of the poem herself, it will be contagious. "I came across this poem that I like a lot, and I wanted to share it with you." A children's librarian or a good children's book store can help you find collections of excellent children's poetry, both "classic" and contemporary. You will find that if you use a lot of poetry with children they will begin to generate their own delightful poems.

Early Literacy

Books

All kinds of books are interesting to five-year-olds, especially humorous story books, books where animals take on the roles of people, and factual books that tell them about their world. Since fives love to know how things work, they love the many excellent, illustrated children's books that show the insides of buildings, machines and vehicles. Pictured dictionaries and encyclopedias are another popular choice.

Regular trips to the library are highly recommended. The child can get the sense of the wonderful variety of books out there, and she'll also see many adults enjoying books – good role models. Let the child have the pleasure of browsing and then picking her own books to take home. Help her keep these books special and take good care of them.

Homemade Books

Creating books about their own ideas or experiences is one way to "hook" a child's interest in books. She sees the usefulness of "talk written down." There are many ways to make books. Here's a simple one:

> Sewn Book
>
> *Cut four or five pieces of paper to the same size. A wallpaper sample (books of outdated wallpaper samples are available for free from decorating stores) makes a good cover. Cut it the same size as the paper. Stack these pieces, cover on the bottom, and sew down the middle on a sewing machine.*

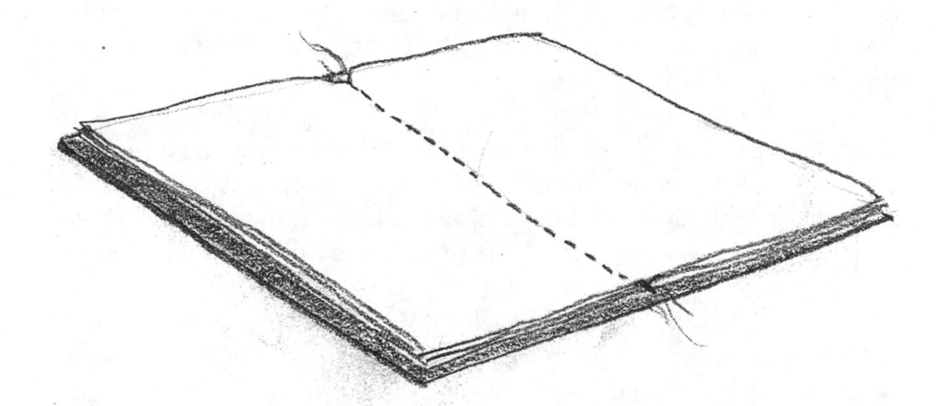

It's a fairly quick process to make a good supply of these. Encourage the child to draw or write about something each day. Write down the child's words for her. For children with more experience, you could print out a short sentence or some words for the child to copy.

Learning to Read

Many five-year-olds have the aptitude to start to learn to read. Most kindergarten programs use a structured reading program. Pre-kindergarten programs, on the other hand, usually teach concepts through more active games and activities. Don't push, though. It won't hurt to wait awhile, and it's best not to frustrate a child. (Children who learn to read later usually catch up with other children by second or third grade.)

Worksheets

Worksheets – workbooks – coloring books – reproducible patterns – are all inappropriate for preschool classrooms. (Preschool is defined as anything under kindergarten level.) For that matter, they're not great for kindergarten either and should be used only in a limited way to provide "drill" for concepts already learned, or allow children to "play school" with them. There are much more effective ways of teaching young children.

Objections to Worksheets

Here are the main objections to using worksheets with preschool children:

• Children this age do not understand abstract concepts well. Letters, numbers and shapes on a piece of paper are abstract symbols representing something else that is real.

• Children learn basic concepts by using all their senses, by manipulating objects. They will not learn anything new with worksheets. At most, worksheets will provide "drill" for concepts already learned.

• Preschool children don't have the fine-motor control to color within the lines, or do many of the other tasks often asked on typical worksheets.

• "Seat work" – sitting at a table doing worksheets is hard enough for kindergarten and first grade students. Younger children have a shorter attention span and find it difficult to sit still for more than a few minutes at a time.

• Worksheets are not fun – not for long, anyway. As soon as the fascination of "playing school" wears off they become drudgery. (Think back to your own days in elementary school. Very few adults remember loving to do workbook pages.) We want to make children eager, enthusiastic learners, not people who avoid learning situations.

• Worksheets do not develop creativity. In some cases they may actively inhibit the creative process in children. When children are given patterns to copy, or color inside the lines, they become less likely to come up with their own ways of drawing things.

• Teachers sometimes use worksheets merely to "occupy" children – to use up time. There are so many better things children can be doing with their time.

Alternatives to Worksheets

Whenever you are tempted to give children worksheets to fill out, ask yourself what purpose you hope to accomplish – what skill you were hoping to teach or reinforce with the worksheet. Then ask yourself how else you might give children that experience without using worksheets. Your alternative is bound to be better.

Listed below are a number of typical worksheet "purposes." We'll examine a number of alternative activities that would accomplish the same goals.

■ Visual discrimination exercises, especially to recognize letter and numeral shapes. *Example:* Circle the letter that repeats:

M B H V N M O W

Alternatives:

Sorting Activities

Give a child a box of assorted seashells. Pick out one and ask the child to find all the others that are the same kind. Do the same with buttons, socks, nuts, assorted dried beans, etc. (Children must notice details, likenesses and differences.)

Find the Letter

Affix letters or numerals to a table top with clear contact paper. Then hand a child a letter cut-out and let the child find the one that is the same.

Magazine Letter Hunt

Give the child an old magazine and let him cut out examples of the letter or numeral you designate and paste them onto another sheet of paper.

Circle the Letter

Let the child find and circle letters or numerals on a newspaper page. Give the child a magnifying glass to make it more fun.

Letter Sorter

Glue different letters or numerals in sections of egg cartons. Glue matching letters inside bottle caps. The child puts the bottle caps in the egg carton sections with the matching letters or numerals.

- Associating upper case and lower case letters. *Example:* Draw lines to connect upper and lower case letters:

s G
d K
g S
a D
k A
x X

Alternative:

Letter Checkers

Glue upper case letters to squares on a checkerboard. Glue lower case letters to checkers. The child places the checker on the square with the corresponding upper case letter.

- Associating letters with initial sounds. *Example:* Circle the letter with the same beginning sound as "bottle:"

D B T H G

Alternatives:

Alphabet Clothesline

Attach a clothesline to a wall or divider where children can easily reach it. Put four or five letters on the wall over the clothesline. Have an assortment of objects that represent the letters on the wall with their beginning sounds and some clothespins. The child attaches the object that has the same initial sound under the letter.

Picture Letter Match

Divide a large piece of posterboard into a number of squares. Put a different letter on each square. On smaller squares of posterboard that will fit inside the squares on the large piece, paste pictures to represent the sound of each letter on the board. The child must try to place each picture in the correct square.

Grandma's Bag Game

Spread out on the floor several pieces of paper with individual letters written on them. In a bag or suitcase, have several objects that represent those letter sounds. Children reach in and take out one object at a time and place it on top of the appropriate letter on the floor.

- Learning shapes.

  Alternatives:

  Shape Hunt

  Find objects in the room of the shape you are talking about. ("Plant" some if necessary.)

  Use manipulatives or homemade toys that emphasize shape concepts.

- To make classroom decorations that go along with a theme unit you are working on with children.

  Alternatives:

  If you're learning about airplanes, for instance, visit an airport, and put pictures and books about airplanes in the room for children to see. If they happen to draw airplanes in their spontaneous art work, great. If not, don't worry about it. Coloring in an outline of an airplane will not teach a child a thing about airplanes.

- To "test" children to see if they know certain concepts.

  Alternatives:

  Simply ask children, or play games such as those just described.

- To inform parents about what children are learning.

  Alternatives:

  Talk to parents directly. Write notes. At a parent conference or parent night have their own children demonstrate how to play the games. In a parent newsletter, suggest games for parents to play at home with their children that will reinforce concepts being learned at the center.

COGNITIVE DEVELOPMENT

The five-year-old has made a big leap in thinking. Preschoolers are mainly creatures of the here and now. But five-year-olds commonly think and talk about what they're going to do tomorrow, or later in the day, and what they did yesterday. There is more planning and reflection. They like to talk about when they were babies, and when they will be big like their teen-aged brothers.

They are also able to think in a "what-if" mode, about things that have not really happened, but might. This is very useful in problem solving. They can understand cause and effect and think of ideas and possible solutions to problems.

Their understanding of space and geography is still sketchy. Parents of Richard, a bright kindergarten boy, decided to take him to visit his grandmother who lived England, in an apartment outside of London. They prepared him by showing him a globe and tracing the route of the airplane. They read books and showed him pictures of England. Several days after they arrived, they decided to "do the sights" in London. After hours of going from one museum to another, Richard got tired and asked if they could please just go back to "England." He thought England was his grandmother's apartment house. "Grandmother lives in England."

Try having the child create a map of her room, or her back yard or neighborhood or school. Representing something three-dimensional on a flat piece of paper is a difficult thing to do, but it is an interesting project, with adult help. You might also let the child make a three-dimensional "miniature" model of the space, using a box, blocks, etc.

Math Concepts

Many kindergarten programs have some type of structured math program for children. Again, especially for pre-kindergarten children, try to think of alternatives to worksheets for learning math concepts.

There are many different processes involved in learning to understand the system of mathematics. Making and repeating patterns, grouping like objects together into "sets," understanding "one to one correspondence" – touching each object once as you count – rote counting to learn the sequence of numerals, understanding comparisons, sequencing – ordering things from small to large, etc. And we haven't even begun to talk about addition and subtraction.

There are mathematical concepts you can incorporate into

simple day-to-day living. Setting the table, children will have to put down one plate for each child (one to one correspondence) and one fork for each plate, etc. The child will have to count how many people are present to know how many plates to get. Are there more children here today than yesterday? How many more?

Making graphs of all types shows children some of the uses of math. How many people have blue eyes in your class? How many have brown eyes? Green eyes? Put these on a graph and then compare the numbers. Which line has the most? The least? Make graphs about the weather, about what kinds of pets classmates have, about favorite musicians, about how many buttons people have on their clothes that day, about their favorite flavor ice cream, etc., etc., etc.

Cooking projects give children many practical experiences with mathematics – measuring, counting, weighing, timing, etc. And don't forget the final product – dividing, passing out portions and eating!

Time

Five-year-olds understand most of the abstract concepts of space and time. They know the days of the week, the months, the season.

This is the ideal age to do "calendar activities," reinforcing names of days and months, counting, and experiencing left to right progression. It's also a good context for learning ordinal numbers: first, second, third, etc.

They also benefit from playing with hour glasses, egg timers and stopwatches. Most five-year-olds cannot tell time except in a rudimentary way.

The Urge to Find Out

Five-year-olds will enjoy a well-developed science table, and will eagerly learn new words connected with science. They really want to know more about how the world works.

Going on a variety of field trips will broaden their understandings. Nature centers, zoos, an auto repair shop, a bakery, are examples of interesting trips with a focus on science.

Books about insects, birds, mammals, etc. will be of great interest. Those published by National Geographic and Dorling Kindersley are particularly fine. *Ranger Rick* magazine, published by the National Wildlife Federation and *World* magazine, published by National Geographic, provide a wealth of stimulating information. There are also many good resource books on science topics for teachers.

MUSIC

Five-year-olds enjoy all types of music activities. Group singing, dancing, and rhythm band instruments will attract eager participation.

Knowing the words to the same songs and singing them together is a socially bonding experience children love. Create a song book with copies of children's favorite songs so that you remember to sing them often. Ask parents if they would like a copy so they can sing along at home.

Rhythm Band Orchestra

Fives can really have fun with rhythm instruments if you show them some different things to do. Try setting them up "orchestra style" with similar instruments grouped together. Then "conduct" them, indicating with your hands when to play loudly and softly, and when certain sections should start and stop. Then, of course, when they get the idea, choose a child to be the conductor.

With their increased memory skills, they may even enjoy learning some simple "dance routines." This is an excellent cognitive activity using the whole body, involving memory, and sequencing. It can be a fun way to expose children to music of different cultures as well.

HOW THEY PLAY

"Cooperative Play" is the norm for five-year-olds. They usually prefer playing with one or more other children to playing by themselves. They assign roles, "set the scene," get ideas from each other, and can get quite involved in their play scenario. This is most obvious when they are involved in dramatic play in the dress-up corner. But it happens outside on the climber and on wheeled toys, while playing with blocks, and while building with construction toys as well.

Children doing art projects will engage in pleasant social conversations while sitting at the same table with others. It is distressing to see kindergarten programs which are so "business like" or limited for time that they think blocks, dress-up play and outside play are a waste of time. It is in these activities that children's imaginations flourish, providing them ultimately with a greater flexibility in thinking and coping skills.

Dramatic Play

Like four-year-olds, fives enjoy a wide range of dramatic play opportunities. Develop props to represent many different roles for children to act out in spontaneous dramatic play.

They also enjoy acting out familiar stories and putting on simple plays. You could make stick puppets to represent the characters of a familiar story. Children hold them up as you read, when that character talks in the story. Then let children act out the same story playing the characters rather than using puppets.

Creative Play

Art activities are very popular, and drawings and paintings are often accompanied by stories. The teacher or parent should be ready to take dictation from the child, writing down her words. How wonderful to be able to read words you thought of yourself!

Unlike a four-year-old who typically recognizes something in a random scribble and names it, a five-year-old will usually decide ahead of time what she wants to draw. Drawings become more representational – rather than messing around with the materials in a random way, the child seeks to make a drawing of something recognizable. You see such things as houses, cars and animals.

Her drawings of people are becoming more realistic. Instead of legs and arms coming out of a big head, there is usually a body now, and the head is smaller, more in proportion. More and more details appear as time goes on – fingers, hair, clothing, buttons, etc.

Children do not need to be taught how to draw. Do not make critical comments about children's representations or try to "correct" the drawing in any way. This type of "instruction" is much more likely to inhibit creativity rather than enhance it.

Concentrate on providing children with a wide variety of materials. Expose them to many different art processes. Collage, printing, wax resist, ink, wet chalk, water colors in trays, and tempera paint, all broaden the child's creative and expressive potential. An art shelf where children can help themselves and carry out their ideas is an added plus to a kindergarten or pre-kindergarten program.

Collect pictures and books with interesting and beautiful illustrations to develop children's sense of aesthetics. When you select books from the library, look for books with beautiful illustrations as well as stories which will appeal to children.

Constructive Play

When children play with blocks, wood, clay and other constructive materials, they typically make something they can then play with. Animals and people fashioned from clay acquire voices and personalities. Whole cities emerge in the sand box. Blocks turn into buildings and towns. Children enjoy working together on such projects.

Games with Rules

Simple games that allow children to show off their growing motor skills, such as hopscotch, can be fun. They can also find success with simple board games, with an adult nearby or as a co-player, to explain the rules. They still find it painful to lose, but are better able to tolerate it than a year ago. They can begin to plan ahead and guess what the other player might be planning to do.

The Play Environment

Time and materials are the essential ingredients. The greater the quantity and variety you offer, the richer the play and creativity will be. In a classroom setting, if children seem to be ignoring certain areas of the room as play choices, change some of the materials that are there. A different kind of glue and new things in the collage box will attract renewed interest. A new bunch of dress-up clothes will create new roles.

Make sure the children have ample time to develop their ideas.

Fifteen minutes after a morning of "seat work" will not be satisfying. They need at least forty-five minutes to develop their ideas and get into their play at more than a superficial level.

Going Outside

Fives still need active play outside. Jump ropes, balls, hoops, parachutes, and other moveable items are very popular with five-year-olds. They can involve themselves in elaborate dramatic play outside, using a climbing structure for a castle or a rocket ship. Nature walks, treasure hunts and gardens can provide great learning experiences.

SUMMARY

The obvious focus of kindergarten and pre-kindergarten programs is "getting ready for school." Don't let your focus on the future ignore the child as she is today. Keep your program fun.

Five-year-olds like to know a lot of facts. Their "why" and "how" questions are legitimate requests for knowledge. Expand their world, building in as many new experiences as you can.

CHAPTER 8

Six- to Eight-Year-Olds

SOMETIMES CALLED "the age of the missing tooth," these are known as the "early middle years" of childhood. Probably the most consistent factor during these early elementary school years is the extreme importance of peers – other children. It's through their relationship to other children that they form their identity, as they put some emotional distance between themselves and their parents and other important adults in their lives.

Children this age are called "industrious." They like to make things, compete with each other, and against themselves, and do real work using real tools. It is during these years that most societies start children in formal schooling or training for later adult roles. Many child care programs care for children of this age before and after school and during the summer. However, if these school-aged children are treated the same as preschool children, we're headed for trouble. Their interests and needs are different, which require a different approach to supervising, teaching and entertaining them.

School-agers also need to feel that what they do is necessary and important. They like to use real equipment rather than toys. Cooking, woodworking, painting, helping with office work, helping other teachers with such things as bulletin boards, even janitorial activities appeal. They are especially responsive when adults express sincere appreciation.

People who work with school-aged children need to be flexible, energetic, resourceful, and interested – an organizer, a teacher of skills, a friend. Some programs stress outdoor activities and sports, while others stress crafts and making things. A balance of both is ideal.

A sense of humor doesn't hurt!

SOCIAL EMOTIONAL DEVELOPMENT

Issues of Emotional Development and Self-esteem

Autonomy

Children this age like to do things by themselves and manage themselves from time to time. This is an important need to take into consideration. Giving kids lots of choices of things to do, letting them structure their own time, decide what they want to do, form their own groups, initiate activities teachers didn't suggest, and take an active part in planning classroom activities and routines help accommodate this need. It is very important to allow a child to choose not to do an activity that is offered. Youngsters who are over-supervised, directed too closely, "dominated" by the teacher, will rebel.

Relationship to Adults

The relationship to the adult in charge is different for school-agers than it was for preschool children. Younger children have great emotional dependence on their caregiver and the majority of their interactions are with the caregiver. With older children, the role of the adult is less central in the child's interactions. Instead of looking to the adult for gratification, school-aged children look to each other. The role of the adult must shift accordingly from one of nurturer and entertainer to one of facilitator and supporter. The adult should assist the group in planning what would be fun and help them get the materials they need. Arrange time and space to give children a wide choice of activities. Be available to act in a supportive role in children's problem solving and conflict resolution processes.

Make no mistake. Children still love their parents and can have warm relationships with other adults. But they have become part of the wider world. This world is full of other children their age. There is a strong drive to "fit in." As they measure themselves against other children they develop their sense of self-worth.

Relationships with Other Children

The peer group emerges as supreme at this age. Interaction with friends of about the same age takes on significant importance for the child. Contact with other children provides for the give and take experiences that allow children to develop their own styles and personalities. There will be leaders – the "popular" ones. These are usually children who are good looking, strong, witty or have some other strong characteristic that attracts others to them. Some children will do almost anything to gain the acceptance of other children, such as wearing only a particular type of clothing, cutting their hair a certain way, or engaging in acts designed to impress.

Clubs

Middle-years children like to form cliques and clubs with their peers. Groups such as this are constantly forming and re-forming. They often spend more time organizing the club and discussing rules, roles, and the status of individual members than actually doing anything. The guidance of an adult can turn the negative aspects of cliques into the positive aspects of clubs and give clubs the means and subtle direction to actually accomplish something as well. This is probably one reason for the success of traditional programs, such as scouting, for this age. Some school-age child care programs take advantage of this interest and are organized as "clubs" with "governments." This can work really well if the adult acts as the advisor and not the leader of the whole operation. Allow them to make up their own roles, rules, and procedures, within reason. Most important, let them plan activities they would like to do. It is a good idea to encourage frequent re-elections with short terms to allow different children to try different roles and experience leadership.

Help children gain a sense of identity with their "club." Uniforms serve this function with scouts. Perhaps you can decorate your own club T-shirts. Club handshakes, secret pass words, codes, etc. help accomplish this goal. The end result is a feeling of belonging.

Children can be divided into smaller "sub-groups" from time to time, perhaps as a way of signing up for a special activity. Try forming special interest groups such as a needlepoint club or a cooking club which a limited number can sign up for that will be in existence for a few weeks while new skills are learned.

Same Sex Preference

Children between the ages of six and nine years usually choose to play with someone of their own sex. This is by no means rigid. Boys seem more preoccupied with the "male role" than girls are with the female role. Try to keep gender stereotyping out of your activities. Recognize that boys may enjoy jewelry making and cooking, and girls will enjoy carpentry and playing ball. Keep activities open to both sexes.

Excluding Others

Belonging to the group has two features – belonging and excluding. While children strive to fit in and have lots of friends, it seems almost as important to them to determine who does not belong. Children can be cruel in their teasing and taunting and scapegoating of certain targeted children. It presents a real dilemma for adults, because the more an adult stands up for the child, it seems, the stronger the dislike of the other children. It takes sensitivity, and there are some subtle things a caregiver can do to help a child gain acceptance and feel like an important part of the group.

Model being a good friend yourself. Give each child a friendly greeting and make time to talk to kids individually, just asking about school, and what's going on in their lives. Be interested, without being judgmental. If the others sense that you like a person, they are more likely to be friendly toward that person themselves. However, be careful not to create a "teacher's pet" situation where you favor one child and build resentment in the others.

You can plan activities that are comfortably done in a small, social group. Let children choose many of their own activities, and with whom they will do them much of the time. You can, however, "engineer" certain relationships, setting up an activity so that two children do something together and get acquainted in the process. It's easier to be friends when they discover common interests.

It seems really hard for children to play well together in groups of three. When three children play together for any length of time, two of them almost inevitably gang up against the third child. You can avoid this somewhat by not grouping children in threes. It's much easier for them to function well in pairs or bunches.

You may be able to help children gain social skills by "coaching" in certain situations. If you become aware of certain behaviors that turn other children off, you can quietly make the child aware, and help him plan other strategies.

Solitude

While fitting in with the group is very important, children this age may also need some time to get away from the gang and be by themselves, especially after having been part of a large group of children in school all day. A little solitude, when self-chosen, might present some needed relief.

Is there a nook in your room you could fix up with a light, a rug and some pillows where a child could be permitted to go by himself? Perhaps you could rig up some "one-person-spaces" in your room using large boxes or furniture to block off a small corner, or even a small tent. Some children need this more than others.

Typical Behavior Issues

Many people list "discipline" as one of the more difficult aspects of working with this age. What caregivers are usually talking about is helping children get along with each other in a way that takes the rights and feelings of others into consideration, as well as treating adults with respect.

Rules and Fairness

Children should be involved in setting rules for the classroom and its various procedures and routines. Specific guidelines for behavior give them a sense of security and comfort. Do realize, however, that school-aged children judge each other more harshly than would adults, so the teacher will have to ensure that rules remain simple, fair, enforceable and consistent. The child learns and applies the rules of right and wrong in a way that makes no allowance for good intentions and extenuating circumstances. "Fairness" is a major preoccupation of this age group. "Fair" means "equal" to them. Everyone should get the same amount, and be treated the same, according to their thinking.

Aggression

At the top of the list of troublesome behaviors is aggression. Children this age have a very narrow understanding of "fairness." That understanding drives them to "even the score." Many fights occur when one child tries to "get even" with another child for something. Furthermore, they sometimes do not understand the accidental nature of some acts which might seem like aggression but are really not intentional. For instance, one child does a somersault and accidentally kicks a second child. The second child may have a strong desire to hit or otherwise hurt the somersaulter, even though it was an accident. It helps to teach them to say quickly, "I didn't mean to hurt you...it was an accident." It may also help "even the score" if you can convince the person who committed the accident or aggression to help the victim. Getting the victim a cold cloth, or helping rebuild or remake something destroyed could help.

Competition

Competition is a fact of life for this age, like it or not. Children are always comparing how their work or skill stands up compared to someone else's.

They like to win. You will not eliminate competition by banning games or sports. The adult can have a significant influence on how youngsters take winning and losing. Giving praise for a "good try" or a "game well-played," as well as for winning, can have a positive effect on how they feel about themselves. The adult can also moderate the behavior of winners. It's OK to feel good about it, but not to "lord it over" everyone else by bragging.

Ultimately, everyone is good at something. It may not be a sport. Find ways to give recognition for other ways individuals excel, such as handwriting, telling jokes or drawing cartoons.

Young people this age group also enjoy competing against themselves, and "setting personal records." Timers and stop watches provide opportunities to compete with themselves, and can add new challenges to mundane activities.

One good book of games enjoyed by middle-years children is *The Outrageous Outdoor Games Book,* by Bob Gregson (Pitman Learning, Inc.).

GROSS MOTOR DEVELOPMENT

Children this age are developing physical skills rapidly, although the rate of growth has slowed down a bit in comparison to the preschool years. Developing skills and gaining mastery are dominant drives of the school-ager. Skill building activities of all types are popular, including all kinds of sports, skating, bike riding and active games such as hula hoops, jump rope, hopscotch, etc. Special trips to such places as a skating rink or bowling alley are very popular.

Their ability to feel capable with new physical skills can also be closely connected with their development of self-esteem. Some children are quite good at physical tasks, and learn easily. Others may be awkward and clumsy due to uneven physical growth. For this reason, it is important to try to help each child gain skills, or find an activity at which he can excel. A child who may be poor at ball playing could be an excellent swimmer, or very good at some fine-motor skill.

Stunts

These children like to test their abilities, take risks, show off and dare each other in a show of bravado. For this reason, even though they may seem very capable, they still require supervision and an occasional adult-imposed limit. Make sure playground equipment is kept in good repair.

Energy

Children this age are typically very energetic and enjoy strenuous physical activity. Do take care to provide a balance in the day. Children who have been cooped up in a very structured school situation all day will need to blow off steam and run and yell when they first arrive in the afternoon. On the other hand, a full day program, during a vacation week, will need a balance of quiet time activities.

Food

School-aged kids always seem to be hungry. It would be wise to acknowledge and anticipate this. Provide generous and nourishing snacks and lots to drink. The afternoon will go much more smoothly and everyone will be in a better mood. This is one reason cooking projects are very popular in many school-age programs.

FINE MOTOR DEVELOPMENT

Enjoyment of mastering new skills applies to fine-motor activities as well. Games such as jacks and cat's cradle, and developing skill in a craft such as knitting and knot tying are examples. Learning sign language has been a favorite activity of some school-age programs, involving both fine-motor skills and the cognitive activity of using symbols in new ways.

LANGUAGE DEVELOPMENT

The main structures of language are mastered and children are able to communicate well. Now they enjoy playing with language – doing stunts, so to speak, just as they do with their gross-motor skills. Tongue twisters, puns, word play, codes, rhyme, ritual chants that go with games are examples. This is a good time to expose children to rich and fun poetry, such as that of Shel Silverstein. See if you can find a book of limericks or other fun poetry as well.

While children understand many words, they are still quite literal in their thinking and often miss subtle meanings or associations in some of our popular expressions. Try asking children what some sayings mean, such as "Every cloud has a silver lining," "Absence makes the heart grow fonder," or "A bird in the hand is better than two in the bush." You're likely to get some interesting interpretations. For this reason, books such as *Too-Loose the Chocolate Moose* by Stewart Moskowitz (Simon and Schuster, 1982) are fun.

This is the ideal time for children to learn a second language. Their brains are still "elastic" in the language area – flexible and able to absorb new sounds and patterns. And because a foreign language can be a kind of "code" or game, the children usually find it enjoyable. When children learn a second language in childhood and forget it because of lack of continuity, they will be able to "relearn" it more easily later on.

Early literacy

In school, children are busy learning to read. You have an opportunity to encourage a love of reading by providing opportunities in a fun environment, free of pressure and tests. Build a cozy library corner with a wide variety of books and magazines that appeal to this age. Joke and riddle books, cartoon books, and magazines written for this age which feature animals and stories about other children, invite children to read just for the fun of it.

Even though children can read themselves, they still love being read to. Find some exciting chapter books and read a little to children every day. A children's librarian can give you some good suggestions. Recorded books are another option to help children enjoy books. If you have a listening station with headphones, this gives children a little "solitude" experience in the group, sometimes just what a child needs to calm down and relax. While children are not "reading" *per se* in these activities, they are enjoying a well-told story, learning to think about characters and follow the sequencing of the plot, hearing rich language, and seeing the usefulness of books for entertainment as well as information.

Provide lots of writing equipment – pencils, pens of all types, and a good supply of paper easily available to children to use in their various creative projects and dramatic play. Word processing computer software can encourage creative expression as well.

You could create a book-making station where children can write down and illustrate jokes, poems, diaries, stories, etc. You might have a number of blank books made up ahead of time, or provide the materials so children can make them themselves. You could also add a typewriter, printing stamps of letters, and art materials of all kinds, along with regular writing materials listed above.

COGNITIVE DEVELOPMENT

The child of this age has made considerable progress in thinking skills, more and more able to take himself out of the "here and now" and think about things not right in front of him, or perceivable with the senses. He slowly, and somewhat reluctantly, comes to realize that the world existed before he was born, and even considers the idea that his grandmother was once a little girl. And he can think about places he has not seen.

The child's social sphere is also influenced by the growing ability to think in more abstract ways. The school-aged child is less egocentric than preschool children. He is more able to consider another's point of view. Negotiating – "I'll do this for you if you do that for me," and trading become easier strategies to use in settling disputes.

His more than five years of experience playing with objects has enabled him to put things into categories, sometimes sorting by different attributes. For instance, he could sort a pile of clothing by color, then by what they're made of, and later by their uses.

Children can also arrange things in order of some predetermined attributes such as small to large, light to heavy. They might like to arrange outdated paint sample cards from a hardware store by color and ranging from light to dark, for instance, or line up play vehicles in the block corner from small to large.

Scale Game

Provide a simple balance scale (or make one). Let the children gather some random objects such as a book, a shoe, a block, a hat and a plate. First have them guess to arrange the objects in order from lightest to heaviest. Then invite them to check their guesses on the balance scale. Can they figure out how to do this? You could have different objects for them to weigh each day. They learn that the size and shape of the object does not necessarily reflect its weight. Invite them to keep records.

Collections

Many school-aged children develop collections of some sort. These can range from dolls or action figures to trading cards, marbles, stamps, rocks, bottles or pictures of horses. Children seem fascinated by the variety. And they like to amass great numbers of things. This can be encouraged in the classroom, as well as at home. You could develop a "collections corner" and help children think of ways to organize, display and describe their collections. This coordinates with their new interest in sorting and seriating objects described above. You might invite adults with interesting collections to show the children their hobby.

Lists

List-making is another type of collection. How many different kinds of trees or flowers can they identify on a nature walk? How many different kinds of birds come to the feeder outside the window? They also enjoy taking surveys or opinion polls, making a record and compiling data. A "class newspaper" could include some survey conducted by the children each week. It could be anything from favorite snack foods to their opinion of a popular movie or TV show.

Fun with Symbols

It's the age of learning to use symbols. Letters, numbers, musical notes gradually become tools to represent ideas. Of course, this goes on for years and has to do with their ability for more abstract thinking and the idea that one thing can represent something else. It had its beginning in the earlier years when children used objects to represent something else in their dramatic play. Now they are ready to learn to use the symbols of society – letters and numbers, as well as other symbols.

Generally, they like to create their own symbols – a kind of "in group" communication.

<u>*Flags for Routines*</u>

You could talk about how a flag is a symbol and show children various types of flags, including the old Signal Corps flags. Then suggest they create their own flags to represent different elements of their routines, such as clean-up time, snack time, going outside time, quiet time, etc. Give them fabric and paint to use. These flags could be raised by designated people at appropriate times, and it frees the adult from being "bossy" and telling kids what to do all the time.

<u>*Codes*</u>

Talk about what a code is and invite them to make up their own codes. You could start by showing them the Morse Code. Then suggest they create a new symbol for each letter of the alphabet and write a note to a friend.

<u>*Rebus Stories*</u>

Show the children some simple rebus stories (where a picture symbol replaces certain words or syllables). These can often be found in children's magazines. Then create their own stories or messages this way.

<u>*Maps*</u>

A map is a system of symbols – two-dimensional designs to represent spaces and places. Show children all kinds of maps and then invite them to make simple maps of familiar places such as their room at home, their child care center, the playground, etc. It might be fun for them to create a treasure map for their friends to show where that day's snack is hidden.

Games with Rules

Games are very popular with this age group. Whether they are board games like checkers or battleship, card games, word games, or active games, school-agers enjoy competing in this way. They gradually learn to imagine what the other player is thinking or planning. A "Games Center" in a classroom or child care setting is always a good idea.

Tournaments are a type of collection. Children like to play a game over and over, trying to see how many points they can earn over a period of time or how many times they can win in a week. You could also ask if they would like to make up their own games. Rules could be discussed and changed with consensus of the group. Games with rules require that one child must put himself in others' shoes.

Organized sports are often the choice of children this age, with a lot of prodding from parents. They can be very positive for children, giving them experiences of belonging to a team and working together to build skills under the influence of interested adults. It's critical that the adults involved put the child first, over the pleasures of winning, and that no child feels left out or less worthy because of his lower skill level. Striving toward a goal and improving abilities should always be balanced with reasonable achievement goals, and care should be taken so that the child does not feel stressed.

Electronic games are extremely popular with this age group. Their value depends upon the particular game. Adults should monitor children's choices and avoid games depicting violence. Many electronic games are solo activities, and while they may help children pass time, they have none of the social advantages of other types of games.

MUSIC

Having a feeling of belonging is very important to school-aged children. One way children can gain this sense of being part of a distinct group is for everyone to know the words to the same songs. There are many resources available. One favorite is *Wee Sing Silly Songs* by Pamela Conn Beall and Susan Hagen Nipp (Price/Stern/Sloan Publishers). This particular collection contains the words to many of the childhood and camp songs remembered by adults, a good place to start.

This is the ideal time for children to learn to play a musical instrument. Their ability to use symbols makes it possible to learn to read music, and their increasing fine-motor ability makes it easier to use their fingers on the instruments to create sounds. It would be great to have a variety of instruments available from time to time for children to explore freely, after someone demonstrates how they are played.

Musical Symbol Game

First have the group come up with three or four different sounds they can make with their mouths or bodies. Then decide on a symbol for each. Then arrange them on a chart in a pattern and let the kids "perform" this silly sound pattern. Also develop signals for loud and soft and "freeze." A fun way to laugh together, it also lets children think about the symbols of standard music notation, which you could weave in later on.

Clap: ⌇ *Raspberry:* ▓ *Meow:* ∿ *Bark:* ||

Dancing

This age group also likes to imitate teenage dancing. You might institute a "Friday dance time" and invite children to bring music, or use a popular radio station. But don't stop there. Line dancing, square dancing and folk dancing are also great fun, and allow children to learn and repeat patterns using their whole body – cognitive and motor skills.

HOW THEY PLAY

Children between six and eight years are wonderful players. They have not yet completely abandoned magic and make-believe, but the line between reality and pretending is sharply drawn. They know when they are pretending, and let others know as well through changes of voice and demeanor and announcements.

They often combine their ability to pretend with their ability to make things and create elaborate structures with blocks or sand, given the opportunity or scenery or props to go along with their fantasy play.

Their make-believe play is likely to be organized with specific roles assigned and sometimes elaborate costumes. They enjoy developing skits and acting in more organized dramas, such as short plays, talent shows, comedic routines, and lip-synching to popular music, complete with plots, scenery and costumes.

They are drawn to gross-motor games that involve some sort of ritual. Many traditional childhood games involve chants such as jump rope rhymes, or particular routines, such as "Mother May I?"

Their play with objects and materials is goal-oriented. They rarely just "mess around" with materials. Instead, they will set about making something specific.

This age is competitive by nature. They like comparing themselves to others and try to "one up" their playmates in stunts and games. Adults need to watch for children's safety in their physical stunts, and also try to find ways for all children to compete successfully in different types of activities emphasizing different skills.

Creative Play

What a wonderful age for creativity! After-school programs can provide many, rich opportunities for creative work, which is often sadly lacking in elementary school programs.

Children this age are very busy learning new skills and love to make things. They need to feel the purposefulness of what they are doing. In sharp contrast to preschoolers, who often care very little about the outcome of their art work, school-agers are very interested in achieving an acceptable final product for their efforts.

Crafts

Craft projects are popular. These are satisfying to children as they follow simple instructions and use developing skills to make something such as a model airplane, a kite, a leather wallet or a needlepoint key chain decoration. Although these projects are not as open-ended as many educators would like, they are not inappropriate for this age. They allow children to read and follow directions and have a sense of pride in accomplishment. You might find resource people in your community to teach such things as crocheting or leather braiding.

"Open-ended" Materials

Be sure to provide many materials that can be used in open-ended ways (with no designated final product) as well, such as paints, yarn, scissors, glue, etc. These are the tools for children's creative ideas. Have a well-stocked art materials shelf where children can find what they need for the various projects they think up. Provide beautiful, quality materials such as rich paint colors and good quality paper, interesting collage materials and glue that works well so that even their "abstract art" is beautiful and satisfying to them. You might offer materials to mat or frame their work. Also allow them to "mess around" with sensory materials such as bubbles and clay.

Salt Paint

Mix equal parts of salt, flour and water to a creamy consistency. Color with tempera paint and pour into squeeze bottles. While younger children like squeezing the bottles to make pools of color, school-aged children have fun creating drawings with this thick paint on a heavy surface like cardboard. It dries overnight into raised, sparkling lines of color.

Colored Glue

Mix tempera paint into small bottles of white glue. Let the children squeeze the colored glue onto card stock such as small pieces of posterboard or large index cards, to make interesting raised designs. When the glue dries they might enjoy coloring in the spaces with felt-tipped marking pens.

Time

These children usually don't mind stretching a creative project over several days in order to complete it, as long as the product is satisfying. Therefore, such projects as woodworking, papier-mâché puppet-making and weaving are good bets. They do, however, demonstrate a real need to complete their projects and get very discouraged if things must be left undone. It helps if teachers break down large projects, which will take several days to complete, into smaller tasks that can be completed in one day. This will provide a feeling of satisfaction at accomplishing something, even though the whole project isn't done yet. For instance, making a papier-mâché dragon could take weeks. The teacher could say, "Today we want to put on one whole layer of papier-mâché that will cover the whole body." Or, "Today we will paint the head." Or, for a needlepoint picture, the child could have a goal of three rows.

Personal Best File

While some children are sensitive about comparing their creative work to someone else's, they can enjoy keeping a file of their own favorites. This could either be a physical file or a bulletin board space for each child in the program. They can decide what to display or put in their file, and what to take out of it. It could include such things as poetry and stories as well as art work. This encourages a child to take pride in his work and notice his own progress.

The Play Environment

One key word is choice. It is difficult to offer today's children the freedom they may have had in generations past when children could roam neighborhoods and ride bikes after school with little or no supervision from adults. However, children this age still need some self-direction and the opportunity to pursue individual interests. A good play environment involves many possible options for play and creativity, and the time and freedom to choose from those options. Children should have a say in what is available.

Indoors

Try to create a balance of energy. Have some cozy areas where a child could choose to curl up with a book or quiet game, as well as areas designated for more active or noisy play. Create nooks where children can be alone, or together with one or two friends, as well as spaces that accommodate a larger group.

Places for make-believe, for construction and making things, art work, board games, books and quiet activities and doing homework, are all possibilities for the indoor environment. Each child should have a place for personal belongings, and places where he can leave unfinished projects.

Going Outside

Lots of space to run and shout and let out their energy is needed for this age group. Hard surfaces for games like hopscotch, jump rope and ball bouncing would be well-used. A basketball hoop is usually in use when available. Large, grassy areas for running and other active games are desirable. Don't forget quiet spots as well – places to sit in the shade with a friend, or tell stories.

SUMMARY

Although there are many models of child care programs for children ages six through eight, most successful programs have several things in common:

• Recognizing the importance of the peer group, a "group identity" is established. The group often has a special name, passwords, etc. and an organization that allow different children to take on leadership roles from time to time. Children have a role in planning what the group will do and in carrying out projects.

• Rather than being a "teacher" in the traditional sense of the word, adults are a combination of facilitator, arbitrator and friend. They are there to help children solve their own problems, get the materials needed to carry out plans, and have a good time with friends.

• Rules are kept to a minimum, but are consistently enforced.

• There is opportunity for sports and games allowing children to compete with each other and learn new skills. Competition is handled lightly, with large doses of encouragement.

• Children are given many opportunities to make things in arts and crafts of all types.

• There are plenty of things to do, and children are allowed to choose what they would like to do or not do.

APPENDIX

Safety Checklist

COMBINE INSATIABLE CURIOSITY, a high activity level and relatively poor coordination and one realizes that young children can hurt themselves on just about anything. The fact that they put everything in their mouths makes choking a major safety concern as well. The most important safety device is close supervision by adults who are really paying attention. Listed here are some basic safety precautions, but don't limit yourself to these. Constantly be alert for any possibly hazardous situation.

INDOORS

- Make sure the environment is free of small objects children could choke on. Objects should be at least the size of a child's fist. Watch especially for toys of older children that may have small pieces dangerous to toddlers.

- Be especially alert for small sharp objects that could cause damage if swallowed, such as safety pins, staples, thumb tacks, paper clips, hair pins, chipped paint, nails, etc.

- Put safety plugs in all electrical outlets not in use. Extension cords are dangerous and should be used *only* for special occasions and under constant supervision. Use masking tape to secure to wall or floor.

- Make sure no appliance cords dangle down where children can pull on them.

- Put safety latches on low cabinet doors and drawers that might contain dangerous substances.

- Make sure toys are in good repair and that there are no sharp edges.

- Do not use glitter because it can scratch the cornea if the child rubs his eyes.

- Do not use balloons with toddlers because if the balloon breaks they can choke on pieces of rubber.

- Tack down loose carpets that could cause beginning walkers to trip and fall.

- Use furniture with rounded edges and maximum stability so that it cannot be tipped over if a child pulls up on it.

- Make sure wooden furniture and toys are free of splinters.

- Train staff and parents not to leave purses in places where children can get into them. They could contain potentially dangerous things such as medications or things to choke on.

- Store all medicine in a locked place totally inaccessible to children. Always keep medicine in original, labeled containers with childproof caps.

- Store all cleaning materials and poisonous substances in a locked cabinet, inaccessible to children. Purchase supplies with childproof tops.

- Post the poison control center phone number at all phones.

- Do not drink coffee or other hot beverages around children. Spilled hot liquids can cause third degree burns.

- Inspect water temperature from hot water faucets and adjust down if necessary. Water should not be warmer than 110 degrees.

- Encourage people to be careful when opening doors and discourage children from playing in front of doors.

- Be very careful when opening and closing doors to make sure no fingers get pinched. If possible, use guards on doors that prevent children from putting their fingers in the crack where they could get pinched.

- Tie cords from blinds or draperies high, out of reach of children.

- Never leave a child unattended on the changing table. In fact, it is good practice to have at least one hand on the child at all times.

- Keep diaper pails covered, and in a place that's inaccessible to babies.

- Check to make sure that any plants in the room are non-toxic, and keep them out of the reach of children.

- Keep cages of any classroom pets clean and the area around them free of debris. Only let children handle animals under the close supervision of an adult.

- Keep sharp objects like scissors and knives out of reach.

OUTDOORS

- Allow children to play only in a securely fenced-in area. The fence should be at least five feet high. The fence should go all the way down to the ground.

- Make sure the fence is in good repair with no gaps where it joins the gate or other places, or bulges at the bottom where children could squeeze through or get stuck.

- Make sure gate latches work well and are out of the reach of children.

- If the fence is made of wood it should be sanded and free of splinters.

- Every time you go outside, check the ground and get rid of any debris or trash that may have blown in since the last time you were outside. Also get rid of natural materials such as acorns or small pine cones that children could choke on.

- Be sure there are no shrubs with thorns or poisonous berries.

- Cover your sand area completely with a sturdy weighted-down cover when not in use to keep out animals.

- Use shock absorbent materials under swings, slides, and climbing equipment to cushion possible falls. These soft surfaces should extend well beyond the equipment, as well as directly under it. The recommended depth depends on the material used (check child care licensing guidelines). Maintain at the proper depth.

- Supervise swings closely. Toddlers cannot predict the path of a swing and will walk right in front of it.

- Use sling type swings with soft seats or horizontal tire swings with toddlers.

- If possible, face slides away from the direct sun so they don't get too hot. Check the temperature of slides before letting children use them. Cool them down with water if necessary.

- Climbing structures should not be too high. Do not place a child on a climbing structure. They should be able to climb up themselves so that they can climb down themselves. Keep toddlers off of climbing equipment designed for older children.

- Check wooden equipment frequently for splinters and sand rough spots when necessary.

- Any gaps in climbers should be four inches or less, or larger than eight inches so the children cannot get their heads stuck in them. Vertical slats are more desirable than horizontal slats, because children always climb on horizontal slats. Any bolts on equipment should be smoothly rounded or recessed to prevent gouges. Make sure there are no sharp edges where children could get cut.

- Makes sure there are no non-play hazards, such as electrical wires or exposed air conditioners or fuse boxes on the playground or that could be reached from climbing structures.

- Protect children's skin from over-exposure to the sun. Sunscreen, hats and bonnets are a good idea.

- Go inside when there is thunder and lightning.

- Do not use wading pools. Even toilet trained children may go to the bathroom in them. You may give each child a small tub or dishpan. Change the water for the next child's use.

- Maintain proper staff ratios at all times, inside and outside.

THESE SAFETY POINTERS ARE NOT MEANT TO BE EXHAUSTIVE. CHECK YOUR CHILD CARE LICENSING GUIDELINES FOR MORE DETAIL AND ADD ITEMS THAT ARE SPECIFIC TO YOUR OWN ENVIRONMENT.